THE MOVING PICTURE GIRLS IN WAR PLAYS

Or, The Sham Battles at Oak Farm

LAURA LEE HOPE

1st WORLD
LIBRARY
Literary Society

The Moving Picture Girls in War Plays

Laura Lee Hope

© 1st World Library, 2007
PO Box 2211
Fairfield, IA 52556
www.1stworldlibrary.com
First Edition

LCCN: 2007934161

Softcover ISBN: 978-1-4218-9658-8
Hardcover ISBN: 978-1-4218-9758-5
eBook ISBN: 978-1-4218-9558-1

Purchase *"The Moving Picture Girls in War Plays"*
as a traditional bound book at:
www.1stWorldLibrary.com/purchase.asp?ISBN=978-1-4218-9658-8

1st World Library is a literary, educational organization
dedicated to:

- Creating a free internet library of downloadable ebooks

- Hosting writing competitions and offering book publishing
scholarships.

Interested in more 1st World Library books? contact:
literacy@1stworldlibrary.com
Check us out at: www.1stworldlibrary.com

1st World Library Literary Society

Giving Back to the World

"If you want to work on the core problem, it's early school literacy."

- James Barksdale, former CEO of Netscape

"No skill is more crucial to the future of a child, or to a democratic and prosperous society, than literacy."

- Los Angeles Times

"Literacy... means far more than learning how to read and write... The aim is to transmit... knowledge and promote social participation."

- UNESCO

"Literacy is not a luxury, it is a right and a responsibility. If our world is to meet the challenges of the twenty-first century we must harness the energy and creativity of all our citizens."

- President Bill Clinton

"Parents should be encouraged to read to their children, and teachers should be equipped with all available techniques for teaching literacy, so the varying needs and capacities of individual kids can be taken into account."

- Hugh Mackay

CONTENTS

CHAPTER I

THE OLD NEWSPAPER

"There, I think I have everything in that I'll need at Oak Farm."

"Everything! Good gracious, Ruth, how quickly you pack! Why, I've oceans and oceans of things yet to go into my trunk! Oh, there are my scout shoes. I've been looking everywhere for them. I'll need them if I do any hiking in those war scenes," and Alice DeVere dived under a pile of clothing, bringing to light a muddy, but comfortable, pair of walking shoes. "I don't know what I'd do without them," she murmured.

"Alice!" cried Ruth, her sister, and the shocked tone of her voice made the younger girl look up quickly from the contemplation of the shoes.

"Why, what have I done now?" came in rather injured accents. "I'm sure I didn't use any slang; and as for not having all my things packed as quickly as you, why, Ruth, my dear, you must remember that you are an exception—the one that proves the rule."

"I didn't say you used any slang, Alice dear. Nor did I

intimate that you were behind in your packing. I'll gladly help you. But it—Those shoes!" and she pointed a finger dramatically at the "brogans," as Alice sometimes called them.

"Those shoes? What's the matter with them? They're a perfectly good pair, as far as I can see; and they're mighty comfortable."

"Oh, Alice—mighty?"

"Well, I can't get over using such words, especially since we heard so many strong expressions from the sailors when we were in those sea films. Mine sound weak now. But what's the matter with the shoes, Ruth?"

"They're so muddy, dear. They will soil all your pretty things if you put them in your trunk in that condition. You don't want that, do you?"

"I should say not—most decidedly! Especially since pretty things with me last about one day. I don't see how it is you keep yours so nice and fresh, Ruth."

"It's because I'm careful, dear."

"Careful! Bosh! Care killed a cat, they say. I'm sure I'm careful, too—Oh, here's that lace collar I've been looking everywhere for!"

She made a sudden reach for it, there was a ripping, tearing sound, and Alice was gazing ruefully at a rent in the sleeve of her dress.

"Oh, for the love of trading stamps!" she ejaculated.

"Alice!" gasped Ruth.

"Well, I don't care! I had to say something. Look at that rip! And I wanted to wear this dress to-day. Oh—"

"That's just it, Alice," interrupted Ruth, in a gentle, chiding voice. "You are too impulsive. If you had reached for that lace less hurriedly you wouldn't have torn your dress. And if you took care of your things and didn't let your laces and ribbons get strewn about so, they would last longer and look fresher. I don't want to lecture—"

"I know you don't, you old dear!" and Alice leaned over— they were both sitting on the floor in front of trunks—and made a motion as though to embrace her sister. But a warning rip caused her to desist, and, looking over her shoulder, she found her skirt caught on a corner of the trunk.

"There! Did you ever?" she cried. "I can't even give you a sisterly hug without pulling myself to pieces. I'm all upset— excited—unstrung—Wellington Bunn doing Hamlet isn't to be compared to me. I must get straightened out."

"I guess that's it—you're all tangled up in your packing," said Ruth, with a laugh. "Truly, I don't mean to lecture, Alice, but you must go a bit slower."

"Not with this packing—I can't, and be ready in time. Why! you are all prepared to go. I'll just throw the things into my trunk and—"

"Now, don't do that. Don't throw things in. You can put in twice as much if you lay the things in neatly. I'll help you. But—oh, dear—!"

Ruth made a gesture of despair.

"What's the matter now? What are you registering?" and Alice used the moving picture term for depicting one of the standard emotions. The girls were both moving picture actresses.

"I'm trying to register dismay at the muddy state of those scout shoes, as you call them, Alice. They may be nice and comfortable, as you say, and really they do look so. And I have no doubt you will find them useful if we have to do much tramping over the hills of Oak Farm. But—"

"Oh, we'll have to do plenty of hiking, as Russ Dalwood warned us," Alice put in. "You know, there are to be several Civil War plays filmed, and they didn't have automobiles or motor cycles to get about on in those days. So we'll have to walk. And it will be over rough ground, so I thought these shoes would be just the thing."

"They will, Alice. I must get a pair myself, I think. But I was just wondering how you got them so terribly muddy. How did you?"

"Oh, Paul Ardite and I were in that Central Park scene the other day. You know, 'A Daughter of the Woods,' and some of the scenes were filmed in the park. It was muddy, and I didn't get a chance to have the brogans cleaned, for I had to jump from the park into the ballroom scene of 'His Own Enemy,' and there was no time. We had to retake in that scene because one of the extras was wearing white canvas shoes instead of ballroom slippers, and the director didn't notice it until the film was run out in the projection room.

"So that accounts for the mud on the shoes, Ruth. But I suppose I can 'phone down to the janitor and have him send them out to the Italian at the corner. He'll take the mud off."

"No, I don't know that you can do that, Alice. We haven't any too much time. If I had an old newspaper, I could wrap the shoes up in that for you, and pack them in the bottom of your trunk. Then the mud wouldn't soil your clothes."

"An old newspaper? Here's a stack of them. Daddy just brought them from his room. Guess he's going to throw them away."

Alice reached up to a table and lifted the top paper from a pile near the edge. She opened it with a flirt of her hand and was about to wrap the muddy shoes in it when some headlines on one page caught her attention. She leaned eagerly forward to read them, and spent more than a minute going over the article beneath.

"Well," remarked Ruth finally, with a smile, "if you're going to do that, Alice, you'll never get packed. What is it that interests you?"

"This, about a missing girl. Why, look here, Ruth, there's a reward of ten thousand dollars offered for news of her! Why, I don't remember seeing this before. Look, it's quite startling. A San Francisco girl—Mildred Passamore—mysteriously disappears while on a train bound for Seattle—can't find any trace of her—parents distracted—they've got detectives on the trail—going to flood the country with photographs of her —all sorts of things feared—but think of it!—ten thousand dollars reward!"

"Let me see," and in spite of the necessity for haste in the packing, Ruth DeVere forgot it for the moment and came to look over her sister's shoulder to read the account of the missing California girl.

"It is strange," murmured Ruth. "I don't remember about that.

I wonder if she could be around here? The New York police are wonderful in working on mystery cases."

"But the funny part of it is," said Alice, "that I haven't noticed anything about it in the New York papers. Have you? This is a San Francisco paper. Naturally they'd have more about it than would the journals here. But even the New York papers would have big accounts of such a case, especially where such a large reward is offered."

"That's so," agreed Ruth. "I wonder why we haven't seen an account of it in our papers. I read them every day."

"What's that? An account of what? Have the papers been missing anything?" asked a deep, vibrating voice, and an elderly man came into the girls' room and regarded them smilingly.

"Oh, hello, Daddy!" cried Alice, blowing him a kiss. "I'm almost ready."

"Hum, yes! You look it!" and he laughed.

"It's this, Daddy," went on Ruth, holding out the paper. "We were going to wrap Alice's muddy shoes in this sheet, when we happened to notice an account of the mysterious disappearance of a Mildred Passamore, of San Francisco, for whom ten thousand dollars reward is offered. There has been nothing in the New York papers about it."

Mr. DeVere, an old-time actor, and now employed, with his daughters, by a large motion picture concern, reached forth his hand for the paper. He gave one look at the article, and then his eyes went up to the date-line. He laughed.

"No wonder there hasn't been anything in the New York

papers of to-day about this case," he said. "This paper is four years old! But I remember the Passamore case very well. It created quite a sensation at the time."

"Poor girl! Was she ever found?" asked Ruth.

"Why, yes; I believe she was," said Mr. DeVere, in rather dreamy tones. He was looking over other articles in the paper.

"Who got the reward?" asked Alice.

"Eh? What's that?" Her father seemed to come back from a mental journey to the past.

"I say, who got the reward?"

"What reward?"

"Why, Daddy! The one offered for the finding of Miss Passamore. The girl we just told you about—in the paper—ten thousand dollars. Don't you remember?"

"Oh, yes. I was thinking of something else I just read here. Oh, the reward! Well, I suppose the police got it. I don't remember, to tell you the truth. I know that her disappearance at the time created quite a sensation."

"And are you sure she was found?"

"Oh, yes, quite sure. Look here!" and with a smile on his face he leaned forward, one rather fat finger pointing to the article he had just been reading. "I was wondering how you girls got hold of this old back-number paper, but I see it's one of several I saved because they had printed notices of my acting. This is a very good and fair criticism of my work when I was appearing in Shakespearian drama—a very fair notice, ahem!" and Mr. DeVere leaned back in his chair, a gratified smile on his face.

"A fair notice! I should say it was!" laughed Alice. "It does nothing but praise you, and says the others offered you miserable support."

"Well, it was fair to *me*," said Mr. DeVere. "Yes, I remember that tour very well. We were in California at the time of this Miss Passamore's disappearance. Helen Gordon was my leading lady then. Ah, yes, that was four years ago."

"No wonder there wasn't anything in to-day's New York papers," said Alice. "Well, let me wrap up my shoes, and I'll try to have this packing done in time to get out to Oak Farm."

"Yes, I just stopped in to see how you were coming on," put in her father. "Mr. Pertell wants to get started, and it won't do to disappoint him. There are to be several thousand men and horses in the production, and the bill for extras will be heavy."

"I'll hustle along, Daddy!" cried Alice. "Do you want that paper?"

"No, you may take it. I'll just tear out this page with the theatrical notice of myself."

He handed the remainder of the paper to his daughter, who, with the help of her sister, wrapped up the muddy shoes.

Then the girls proceeded with the putting in of other articles and garments that would be needed during their stay at Oak Farm.

Laura Lee Hope

"I wonder—" began Alice, when there came a knock on their door, and a voice demanded:

"I say, girls!—are you there?"

"Yes, Russ. Come on in!" answered Alice.

"Oh, and with the room looking the way it is!" remonstrated Ruth.

"Can't be helped. Russ knows what packing is," Alice declared, as a tall, good-looking young man entered.

"Come on!" he cried. "No time to lose."

"What's the matter? Is the place on fire?" asked Ruth.

"No. But there's got to be a retake in that last scene of 'Only a Flivver,' and Mr. Pertell sent me to get you. It won't take long, but they're in a hurry for it. Come on! Paul is waiting outside in the machine and I've got the camera. Hustle!"

CHAPTER II

OFF FOR OAK FARM

"What's that, Russ? A retake?" asked Alice.

"Yes, of that auto scene in the park."

"Is that the one I'm in?" Ruth inquired.

"Yes. You're both in it, and so is Paul. It's the scene where Mr. Bunn is struck by the auto mud-guard—not hurt, you know, and you, Ruth, jump out to give first aid."

"What's the matter with the scene?" asked Alice. "I certainly struck him all right with the mud-guard."

"Yes, that part was all right," Russ admitted. Alice had been running the automobile in the scene.

"And didn't I do my first aid business well?" Ruth demanded.

"Yes," Russ acknowledged. "Your part came out perfect. But just at the critical moment—you know, where Mr. Bunn was supposed to think he was dying and wanted to right the wrong he had done in cutting his daughter off in his will with only a dollar—some boys got in the way of the camera. They

Laura Lee Hope

were outsiders, butting in, the way they always do when we film stuff in the park. It wouldn't have been so bad, only one of the youngsters began to pull off some funny stuff right in range of Mr. Bunn's agonized face. I didn't see him at the time, or I'd have stopped the running of the film. It was only when we got it in the projection room that we discovered it.

"So Mr. Pertell ordered a retake of that one scene, and it's got to be done in a hurry. It won't take long. Mr. Bunn will meet us in the park. Be sure and wear the same things you had on that day. It won't do to have you get out of the auto in one dress, Ruth, and, a second later, kneel down beside Mr. Bunn in a gown entirely different."

"All right, Russ, I'll be careful."

"Oh, dear! But my packing!" sighed Alice. "I'll never get it done, and we must start for Oak Farm—"

"Mr. Pertell will have to make allowances," said Russ, quickly. "Come on—move the boat! You won't be needed in the real war scenes for a couple of days, anyhow, though I suppose there'll be rehearsals. But it can't be helped. This retake is holding up the whole film, and it's to be released next week."

Delaying only long enough to put on the proper dresses and to tell their father where they were going, Ruth and Alice DeVere were soon on their way to Central Park, where the scene was to be filmed, or photographed over again—a "retake," as it is called, the bane alike of camera men and directors.

And while the girls—the moving picture girls—are on their way to do over a bit of work, I shall take the opportunity of telling my new readers something about Ruth and

Alice DeVere.

I have called them just what they are: "The Moving Picture Girls," and that is the title of the first volume of this series, which depicts them and their adventures.

Their mother had died some years previously, leaving them to the care of their father, Hosmer DeVere, at one time a talented actor in the legitimate drama. But a throat affection forced him to give up his acting and, at the opening scene in the first volume, we find him and his daughters in rather straitened circumstances, living in a second-rate apartment house in New York.

Across the hall dwelt Russ Dalwood, with his mother. Russ was a "camera man." That is, he took moving pictures in the big studios and out of doors for the Comet Film Company, of which Mr. Frank Pertell was manager and director.

It was Russ who suggested to Mr. DeVere a way out of his troubles. He could not act in the "legitimate," as his voice was gone; but no voice is needed to appear on the films for the movies, since a mere motion of the lips suffices, when any speaking is to be done. The "silent drama" has been the salvation of many an actor who, if he had to declaim his lines, would be a failure.

At first Mr. DeVere would not hear of acting before the camera, but he soon came to know that greater actors than he had fallen in line with the work, especially since the pay was so large, and finally he consented. An account of his success and of the entrance of his daughters into the field is given in the initial book.

Ruth, the elder girl, was, like her father, of a romantic turn. Also she was rather tall and willowy, as Mr. DeVere had been before he had taken on flesh with the passing of the years; and she was cast for parts that suited her type. She was deliberate in her actions, and in "registry."

Alice, like her late mother, was warm-hearted and impulsive, plump, vivacious and full of fun. Both girls were excellent movie actresses. In the company they had joined was Mr. Wellington Bunn, an old actor, who hoped, some day, to appear in Hamlet—Hamlet in the legitimate.

Paul Ardite, who played light parts, had become very fond of Alice. Russ Dalwood had a liking for Ruth, and the four had many pleasant hours in each other's company.

Pearl Pennington was the leading lady at times, and was rather disposed to domineer over our girls, as was her chum, Laura Dixon. Mrs. Maguire was the "mother" of the film company. She portrayed old lady parts, and her two grandchildren, Tommie and Nellie, the orphans, were cast for characters suitable to them.

Carl Switzer, a German-American, did comedy parts and was a good fellow, though occasionally he would unconsciously say some very funny things. His opposite in character was Pepper Sneed, the grouch of the company. But Pepper could do valuable work, especially as a villain, and so he was kept on. As for Pop Snooks, the company could not have got along without him. It was Pop, the property man of the company, who made many of the devices used when the company went to "Oak Farm," as told in the second volume, where scenes for farm dramas were filmed. Pop could use a drawbridge in one scene, and, in the next, convert it into a perfectly good cow-barn. Pop was a valuable man.

There were other members of the company, of more or less

importance, whom you will meet as this story progresses.

It was in the third volume of the series, "The Moving Picture Girls Snowbound," that Ruth and Alice succeeded in getting "the proof on the film" that saved Mr. DeVere from an unjust charge.

From the cold and frostiness of Deerfield the girls went to Florida, where "Under the Palms," many stirring acts were filmed. It was here that Alice and Ruth helped find two girls who were lost in the wilds of the Everglades.

"The Moving Picture Girls at Rocky Ranch" gave Ruth and Alice a taste of cowboy life, and though rivals tried to spoil some of the valuable films, they were not altogether success-ful, even though a prairie fire figured in their schemes.

The girls, with their father, had recently returned from a perilous trip. This is told about in the volume immediately preceding the one you are reading—"The Moving Picture Girls at Sea." In that Alice and Ruth proved, not only their versatility as actresses, but also that they could be brave and resourceful in the face of danger. And they more than repaid the old sailor, Jack Jepson, who saved their lives, by doing him a good turn.

"Well, life at Oak Farm will be vastly different from that on the *Mary Ellen*," remarked Alice, as she looked from the automobile as it swung along through the New York streets on the way to the park.

"Yes," agreed her sister. "But I like it up there."

"There are going to be some strenuous times," said Paul. "We've got to do some hustling work."

"All the better," declared Russ. "I like to keep the film running. This sitting about all day and reeling off only ten feet makes me tired."

"You like action!" laughed Ruth.

"Yes; and plenty of it."

Oak Farm was the property of the Apgars. There was Mr. Belix Apgar, the father, Nance, his wife, and Sandy, an energetic son. The farm was located in New Jersey, about forty miles from New York, and it provided a picturesque background for the scenes evolved by Mr. Pertell and his company. It was during a scene on the farm, some time before, that a valuable discovery had been made, which endeared the moving picture girls and their chums to the Apgars.

"How did Mr. Pertell come to pick out Oak Farm for the war plays?" asked Ruth, as the automobile bounced along.

"Well, I suggested it to him," answered Russ. "I remembered the background, and I felt sure we could get all sorts of settings there to make the proper scenes. There are hills, mountains, valleys, streams, bridges, waterfalls, cliffs and caves. Everything needed for perfectly good war dramas."

"How did they come to want that sort of stuff?" asked Paul.

"Oh, war stuff is going big now," Russ answered. "All this talk of preparedness, you know, the war in Europe, and all that. The public is fairly 'eating up' war pictures."

"I hope we don't have to fire any guns!" exclaimed Ruth, with a shudder.

"You'll see and hear plenty of 'em fired," Russ told her. "There are to be some big battle scenes and cavalry charges. But one of you will be back of the firing line, I believe."

"How is that?" asked Alice.

"Well, one of you girls is to be cast for an army nurse, and the other will be a spy. The spy has to carry a revolver."

"I'm going to be the spy!" cried Alice, impetuously. "I know how to shoot a gun."

"I'd rather be the nurse," murmured Ruth, and truly she was better fitted for that part.

"'A Girl in Blue and A Girl in Gray' is to be the title of the war play—or at least one of them," went on Russ. "There will be some lively scenes, and I'll be on the jump most of the time."

"Are you going to film them all?" asked Paul.

"Oh, no. I'm to have several assistants, but I'll be in general charge of the camera squad. So, girls, look your prettiest."

"They always do that," said Paul.

"Thank you!" came in a feminine duet.

A little later the place where the retake was to be made was reached. Mr. Bunn was on hand, wearing his air of "Hamletian gloom," as Alice whispered, and the work of retaking the scenes was soon under way.

This time all went well. Alice drove her "flivver" at Mr. Bunn, who was properly knocked down and looked after by

Ruth. No small boys, with an exaggerated sense of humor, got in the way, and the girls were shortly back in their apartment. They had moved to a more pretentious home since their success in moving pictures, and the Dalwoods had taken an apartment in the same building.

"And now to get on with my packing!" sighed Alice. "All I am sure of is that I have my 'brogans' in."

"I'll help you," offered Ruth.

Two days later the Comet Film Company, augmented for the occasion, was at the depot in Hoboken, ready to take the Lackawanna train out to Oak Farm, New Jersey, where it nestled in the hills of Sussex County.

"I don't see how they are going to take battle scenes with just this company," observed Alice, as she surveyed her fellow workers. "And where are the guns and horses?"

"They'll come up later," Russ informed her. "There are to be two big companies and a couple of batteries, but they won't be on hand until they are really needed. It costs too much to keep them when they are not working."

"Are you all here?" asked Mr. Pertell hurrying along the seats with a handful of tickets—"counting noses," so to speak.

"All here, I think," answered Russ.

"Where is Carl Switzer?" asked the manager.

"He was here a minute ago," Alice said.

"Well, he isn't here now," remarked Mr. Bunn.

"And almost time for the train to start!" exploded the director. "We need him in some of the first scenes to-morrow. Get him, somebody!"

"Hey, Mister! Does yer mean dat funny, moon-faced man what talks like a pretzel?" asked a newsboy in the station.

"Yes, that's Mr. Switzer," was the answer. "Where is he?"

"I jest seen him go out dat way," and the boy pointed toward the doors leading to the street in front of the ferry. This street led over to the interned German steamships at the Hoboken piers.

CHAPTER III

HARD AT WORK

"Great Scott!" ejaculated Mr. Pertell. "I might have known that if Switzer came anywhere near his German friends he'd be off having a confab with them. Go after him, somebody! It's only five minutes to train time, and it will take those Germans that long to say how-de-do to one another, without getting down to business."

"I'll get him," offered Paul, hurrying off toward the swinging doors.

"I'll go wit' youse," said the newsboy. "I likes t' listen t' him talk. Does he do a Dutch act?"

"Sometimes," laughed Paul.

"Youse is actors, ain't youse?" the boy asked.

"Movies," answered Paul, hurrying along toward the entrance to the shipyards.

"I wuz in 'em onct," went on the lad. "Dey wuz a scene where us guys wuz sellin' papes, an' anudder guy comes along, and t'rows a handful of money in de street—he had so much he didn't know what t' do wit' it—dat wuz in de picture," he explained. "I wuz in de scene."

"Was it real money?" asked Paul.

"Naw—nottin' but tin'," and the tone expressed the disappointment that had been experienced. "But we each got a quarter out of it fer bein' in de picture, so we didn't make out so worse. Dere's your friend now," and the newsboy pointed to the comedian standing at the entrance to one of the piers, talking to the watchman. Both had raised their voices high, and were using their hands freely.

"Hey, Mr. Switzer, come along!" cried Paul. "It's time for the train."

"Ach! Der train! I t'ought der vos plenty of time. I vant to see a friend of mine who is living on vun of dese wessels. Haven't I got der time?"

"No, not a minute to spare. You can see him when you come back."

"Ach! Maybe I neffer comes back. If I get in der war plays I may be shotted."

"Oh, come on!" laughed Paul, while the newsboy went into amused contortions at the exaggerated language and gestures of Mr. Switzer.

"See you later, Hans!" called the comedian to the watchman at the pier.

"Ach, Himmel! Vot I care!" the latter cried. "I don't care even if you comes back neffer! You can't get on dose ship!" and he waved his hand at the big vessels, interned to prevent their capture by the British warships.

"I was having quite an argument with him," said Mr. Switzer, speaking "United States," as he walked back to the station with Paul.

"Wouldn't he let you go on board?"

"No. Took me for an English spy, I guess. But I know one of der officers, and I thought I'd have time for a chat with him."

"Mr. Pertell is in a hurry," said the young actor.

"Well, if we miss this train there's another."

"Not until to-morrow, and he wants to start the rehearsals the first thing in the morning."

"Ach! Den dat's differunt alretty yet again, wasn't it so?" and Mr. Switzer winked at the admiring newsboy, and tossed him a quarter, with the advice to get a pretzel and use it for a watch charm. Whereat the boy went into convulsive laughter again.

"What do you mean, Switzer, by going off just at train time?" demanded the indignant director and manager.

"Train time is der time to go off—so long as you don't go off der track!" declared the German. "But I vanted to go on—not go off—I vanted to go on der ships only dey vouldn't let me. However, better late than be a miss vot's like a bird in der hand," and with a shrug of his shoulders and a last wink at the newsboy, Mr. Switzer went out to the waiting train with the others.

It was a long and rather tedious ride to Oak Farm, which lay some miles back in the hills from the railroad station, and it was late afternoon when the company of moving picture actors and actresses arrived, to be greeted by Sandy Apgar and his father and his mother.

"Well, I *am* glad to see you all again!" cried Sandy, shaking hands with Mr. DeVere, the girls and the others. "It seems like old times!"

"We're glad dot you are glad!" declaimed Mr. Switzer. "Haf you any more barns vot need burning down?"

"Not this time," laughed Sandy. "One barn-burning is enough for me." A barn, an old one, had been destroyed on the occasion of the previous visit of the moving picture company—a burning barn being called for in one of the scenes.

Oak Farm was a big place, and, in anticipation of the war plays to be enacted there, several buildings had been built to accommodate the extra actors and actresses, where they could sleep and eat. The DeVere girls and the other members of the regular company would board at the farmhouse as they had done before.

Hard work began early the next day. There was much to do in the way of preliminary preparation, and Pop Snooks, the property man, with a corps of assistants, was in his element. While Ruth, Alice and the others were going through a rehearsal of their parts without, of course, the proper scenic background, the property man was setting up the different "sets" needed in the various scenes.

While they were working on one piece, Sandy Apgar came along on his way to look after some of the farming operations.

"Hello!" he cried. "Say! you fellows did that mighty quick."

"Did what?" asked Alice, who stood near, not being engaged for the time being.

"Why, dug that well. I didn't know you could strike water so soon," and he pointed to an old-fashioned well with a sweep, which stood not far from the house. "What'd you use—a post-hole digger?" he asked. "What sort of water did you strike?"

Before any one could answer him he strode over to the well, and, as he looked down into it, a puzzled look came over his face.

"Well, I'll be jiggered!" he cried. "'Tain't a well at all! Only an imitation!"

And that was what it was. Some canvas had been stretched in a circle about a framework, and painted to represent stones. The well itself stood on top of the ground, not being dug out at all. It made a perfectly good water-scene, with a sweep, a chain, a bucket and all.

"I'm supposed to stand there and draw water for the thirsty soldiers," explained Ruth, coming up at this point.

"Huh! How are you goin' to git water out of there?" demanded Sandy. "It's as dry as a bone. Why, I've got a good well over there," and he pointed to a real one, under an apple tree.

"That's in the shade—couldn't get any pictures there," explained Russ. "The well has to be out in the open."

"But what about water?" asked Sandy. "Hang me if I ever

heard of a well without water!"

"We'll run a hose up to this one," explained Pop Snooks. "A man will lie down behind the well-curb, where he won't show in the camera. As fast as Ruth lowers her bucket into the well the man'll fill the pail with water for the soldiers to drink. It'll be quicker than a real well, and if we find we don't like it in one place we can move it to another. This is a movable well."

"Well, I'll be—" began Sandy, but words failed him. "This is sure a queer business," he murmured as he strode off.

The hard work of preparation continued. All about the farm queer parts of buildings were being erected, extra barns, out-houses, bits of fence, and the like.

In what are called close-up scenes only a small part of an object shows in the camera, and often when a magnificent entrance to a marble house is shown, it is only a plaster-of-Paris imitation of a door with a little frame around it.

What is outside of that would not photograph; so what is the use of building it? Of course in many scenes real buildings figure, but they are not built for the purpose.

In one of the war plays a small barn was to be shown, and a soldier was supposed to jump through the window of this to escape pursuit. As none of the regular buildings at Oak Farm was in the proper location, Pop Snooks had been ordered to build a barn.

He did. That is, he built one side of it, propping it up with braces from behind, where they would not show. The window was there, and some boards; so that, seen through the camera, it looked like a small part of a big out-building.

Laura Lee Hope

Some hay was piled on the ground to one side, away from the camera, and it was on this hay that the escaping soldier would land. Then Ruth was to come to him, and go through some scenes. But these would be interior views, which would be taken in the improvised studio erected on the farm for this purpose.

Mr. Switzer was to be the soldier, and would plunge through the barn window head first. He was called on to rehearse the scenes a few days after the semblance of a barn had been put in position and the hay laid out to make his landing safe.

"Are you ready?" asked Mr. Pertell, who was directing the scene. "All ready, there, Switzer?"

"Sure, as ready as I ever shall be."

"All right, then. Now, you understand, you come running out of those bushes over there, and when you get out you stop for a minute and register caution. Look on all sides of you. Then you see the barn and the open window. Register surprise and hope. You say, 'Ah, I shall be safe in there!'

"Then you run, look back once or twice to see if you are pursued, and make a dive, head first, through the open window on to the hay. All ready now?"

"Sure, I'm ready!"

"How about you, Russ?"

"Let her go."

"All ready, then! Camera!"

Russ began to grind away at the film. Mr. Switzer had taken

his place in the clump of bushes, his ragged Union garments flapping in the wind. He came out, looked furtively around, and then, giving the proper "registration," he advanced cautiously toward the barn.

"Go on now—run!" cried Mr. Pertell through his megaphone.

The German actor ran. He made a beautiful leap through the window, and the next moment there came from him howls of dismay.

"Donner vetter! Ach Himmel! Ach! My face! My hands! Hey, somebody! bring a pail of water! Quick!"

CHAPTER IV

A REHEARSAL

Mingled in German and English came the shouts of dismay from Herr Switzer inside the dummy shed, through the window of which he had leaped on to the hay.

"Oh, what is it?" cried Ruth, clasping her hands and registering "dismay" unconsciously.

"He must have fallen and hurt himself," ejaculated Alice. "Do, Paul, go and see what it is."

"Stop the camera!" yelled Mr. Pertell through his megaphone. "Don't spoil the film, Russ. You got a good scene there. He went through the window all right, and his yells won't register. Stop the camera!"

"Stopped she is," reported Russ.

Then those of the players who had been looking on and wondering at Mr. Switzer's cries could hurry to his rescue.

For it is a crime out of the ordinary in the annals of moving pictures for any one not in the scene to get within range of the camera when an act is being filmed. It means not only the spoiling of the reel, perhaps, but a retaking of that particular action. When Russ ceased to grind at the camera crank, however, it was the same as when the shutter of an ordinary camera is closed. No more views can be taken. It was safe for others to cross the field of vision.

"What's the matter?" cried Paul, who, with Ruth and Alice and some of the others trailing after him, was hurrying toward the false front of boards that represented a shed.

"Did a cow critter or a sheep step on you?" Russ questioned.

"Ach! My face! My clothes! Ruined!" came in accents of deep disgust from the actor. "Never again will I leap through a window without knowing into what I am going to land. Ach!"

"What happened?" asked Paul, trying to keep from laughing, for the player's voice was so funnily tragic.

"What happened? Come and see!" cried Mr. Switzer. "I have into a chicken's home invaded myself already!"

"Invaded himself into a chicken's home!" exclaimed Mr. Pertell. "What in the world does he mean?"

"I guess he means he sat down in a hen's nest!" chuckled Paul, and this proved to be the case.

Going around to the other side of the erected boards, the players and others saw a curious sight.

Seated on the hay, his face, his hair, his hands, and his clothing a mass of the whites and yellows of eggs, was Carl Switzer. He held up his fingers, dripping with the ingredients of half a dozen omelets.

"The chicken's home was right here, in the hay—where I jumped. I landed right in among the eggs—head first. Get me some water—quick!" implored the player.

"Didn't you see the eggs before you jumped among 'em?" asked Mr. Pertell.

"See them? I should say not! Think you I would have precipitated myself into their midst had I done so?" indignantly demanded Mr. Switzer, relapsing into his formally-learned English. "I have no desire to be a part of a scrambled egg," he went on. "Some water—quick!"

While one of the extra players was bringing the water, Sandy Apgar strolled past. He was told what had happened.

"Plumped himself down in a hen's nest, did he?" exclaimed the young proprietor of Oak Farm. "Wa'al, now, if you folks go to upsettin' the domestic arrangements of my fowls that way I'll have t' be charging you higher prices," and he laughed good-naturedly.

"Ach! Dat is better," said Mr. Switzer, when he had cleansed himself. "How came it, do you think, Mr. Apgar, that the hen laid her eggs right where I was to make my landing when escaping from the Confederates?"

"Huh! More than one hen laid her eggs there, I reckon," the farmer said. "There must have been half a dozen of 'em who had rooms in that apartment. You see, it's this way. Hens love to steal away and lay their eggs in secret places. After you folks built this make-believe shed and put the hay in, I s'pose some of my hens seen it and thought it would be a good place. So they made a nest there, and they've been layin' in it for the last few days."

"More as a week, I should say!" declared Mr. Switzer in his best German comedian manner. "There were many eggs!"

"Yes, you did bust quite a few!" said Sandy, critically looking at the disrupted nest. "But it can't be helped."

"Well, the film wasn't spoiled, anyhow," observed Mr. Pertell. To him that was all that counted. "You got him all right as he went through the window, didn't you, Russ?"

"Oh, yes. It wasn't until he was inside, down behind the boards and out of sight, that the eggs happened."

"No more eggs for me!" declared the comedian. "I shall never look a chicken in the face again."

"Go on with the scene," ordered the director. "You are supposed to steal out to the barn to give the hidden soldier food," he said to Ruth. "You come out from the house, and are astonished to see a man's head sticking out of the shed window. You register surprise, and start to run back to the house, but the soldier implores you to stay, and you reluctantly listen to him. Then he begs for food—"

"But don't bring me a hard-boiled egg, whatever you do!" called Mr. Switzer.

"No funny business now," warned the director, with a laugh. "Go on now, and we'll see how you do it."

After one or two trials Mr. Pertell announced himself as satisfied and the filming of that part of the war drama went on.

So many details in regard to the taking of moving pictures have been given in the previous books of this series that they

Laura Lee Hope

need not be repeated here. Suffice it to say that the pictures of the players in motion are taken on a long celluloid strip of film, just as one picture is taken on a square of celluloid in a snap-shot camera.

This long reel of film, when developed, is a "negative." From it a "positive" strip of film is made, and this is the one that is run through the projection machine throwing the pictures on the white screen in the darkened theatre. The pictures taken are very small, and are greatly magnified on the screen.

So much for the mechanical end of the business. It may interest some to learn that the photo-play, as seen in the theatre, is not taken all at once, nor in the order in which the scenes are seen as they are reeled off.

When a play is decided on, the director or one of his helpers goes over the manuscript and picks out all the scenes that take place in one location. It may be in a parlor, in a hut, on the side of a mountain, in a lonely wilderness, on a battlefield, on a bridge—anywhere, in fact. And several scenes, involving several different persons, may take place at any one of these places.

It can be understood that it would involve a great deal of work to follow the logical sequence of the scenes. That is to say, if the first scene was in an office showing a girl taking dictation from her employer, and the next showed the same girl and her employer on a ferryboat, and the third scene went back to the office, where some papers were being examined, it would mean a loss of time to photograph, or film, the first office scene, then take every one involved in the act to the ferryboat, and then back to the office again.

Instead, the two office scenes, and possibly more, are taken at one time, on the same film, one after the other, without regard to whether they follow logically or not. Afterward the film is cut apart, and the scenes fitted in where they belong.

So, too, all the scenes pertaining to a hut in the wilderness, on a bridge, in the woods, in a parlor—it makes no difference where—are taken at the same time. In this way much labor and expense are saved.

But it makes a queer sort of story to an uninitiated person looking on; and sometimes the players themselves do not know what it is all about.

So Mr. Pertell wanted to get all the scenes centering around the shed at the same time, though they were not in sequence. And Ruth and Mr. Switzer and the others in the east went through their parts with the shed as a background.

In one scene Ruth had to discover the hidden soldier. Then she had to steal out to him with food. Later, at night, she was to help him to escape. Then, a week later, she was to go out to the same shed and discover a letter he had hidden in the hay. That ended the scenes at the shed, and it could be taken away to make room for something else.

"Oh, Ruth, you did that splendidly!" exclaimed Alice, as her sister finished her work and went up on the shady porch to rest.

"Did you like it? I'm glad."

"Like it? It was great! Where you discovered that letter in the hay, your face showed such natural surprise."

"I'm glad it didn't register merriment."

"Why?"

Laura Lee Hope

"Because, as I picked up the letter, I found a big blot of the yellow from the hens' eggs on it. I hope it doesn't show in the picture. I had all I could do to keep from laughing when I thought of Mr. Switzer in the omelet scene."

"Oh, well, you know they want all white stuff yellow when they make pictures."

"In the studio, but not outdoors."

This is a fact. As the scenes in the studio are taken in the glare of a special kind of electric light, all white objects, even the collars and cuffs of the men, are yellow in tone, though in the picture they show perfectly white. This is due to the chemical rays of the lights used. Out of doors, under sunlight, colors are seen in their own hues.

"You did very well in that funny little scene with Paul," said Ruth to her sister.

"You mean in the swing under the apple tree?"

"Yes."

"I was so afraid he would swing me too high," Alice went on. "He was cutting up so. I told him to stop, but he wouldn't."

"It was very natural. I think it will show well. Hark! what's that?" cried Ruth, leaping to her feet.

"Thunder," suggested Alice, as a distant, rumbling noise came to their ears.

"Sounds more like big guns."

"Oh, that's what it is!" agreed Alice. "They are going to rehearse one of the battle scenes this afternoon, I heard Mr. Pertell say. The soldiers must have come, and they're practising over in the glen. Come on over and watch. We're in on the scenes later, but we can watch now."

"All right," agreed Ruth. "Wait until I get my broad-brimmed hat, the sun is hot up here."

Presently the two sisters, with Paul Ardite and some other members of the company, were strolling over the fields toward the scene of the distant firing. As they came in sight of several hundred men and horses, they saw the smoke of cannon and heard the shouting of the director and his assistants who were using big megaphones. It was the rehearsal of one of the many battle scenes that were to take place about Oak Farm.

"Oh, look at that girl ride!" suddenly exclaimed Alice, pointing to a young woman who dashed past on a spirited horse. "Isn't she a wonder?"

"She is indeed," agreed Ruth. "I wonder who she is?"

"One of the extras," said Paul. "A number of them have just arrived. We'll begin active work soon, and film some big scenes with you girls in them."

Alice gazed across the fields toward the figure of the girl on horseback. There was something spirited in her riding, and, though she had never seen her before, Alice felt strangely drawn toward the new player.

CHAPTER V

A DARING RIDER

"Come on now, Confederates!"

"No, you Union chaps hold back there in ambush. You're not to dash out until you get the signal. Wait!"

"Keep that horse out of the way. He isn't supposed to dash across, riderless, until after the first volley."

"Put in a little more action! Fall off as though you were shot, not as though you were bending over to see if your horse had a stone under his shoe! Fall off hard!"

"And you fellows that do fall off—lie still after you fall! Don't twitch as though you wanted to scratch your noses!"

"If some of 'em don't stay quiet after they fall off they'll get stepped on!"

"All ready now! Come with a rush when the signal's given!"

Mr. Pertell and his men were stationed near a "battery" of camera men, who were ready to grind away; and the director and his assistants were calling their instructions through big megaphones. To reach the soldiers in the more distant parts of the field recourse was had to telephones, the wires of which were laid along the ground in shallow trenches, covered with earth so that the trampling of the horses would not sever them.

"Get that battery farther back among the trees!" cried Mr. Pertell to one of his helpers. "It's supposed to be a masked one, but it's in plain sight now. Even the audience would see it, let alone the men it's supposed to fire on. Get it back!"

"Yes, sir," answered the man, and he telephoned the instructions to the assistant director in charge of a battery of field guns that had been thundering away—the sound which had brought Ruth and Alice to the scene.

"Do we have any part in the battle scenes?" asked Ruth.

"Yes, quite big parts," Paul informed her. "But you don't go on to-day. This is only a rehearsal."

"But they've been firing real powder," remarked Alice, "and it looks as though they were going to fire more," and she pointed to where men of the masked battery were ramming charges down the iron throats of their guns.

"Yes, they're firing, and charging, and doing all manner of stunts, and the camera men are grinding away, but they aren't using any film," went on Paul. "It's just to get every one used to working under the excitement. They have to fire the guns so the horses will get so they don't mind them when the real time comes."

Hundreds of extra players had been engaged to come to Oak Farm for these battle scenes in the drama, "A Girl in Blue and A Girl in Gray," and some of them were already on hand with their mounts. As has been said, special accommodations had been erected where they were to stay during the weeks they would be needed. There were more men than women among the extra people, though a number of women and girls were needed in the "town" scenes.

Most of the men were former members of the militia, cowboys and adventurers, all of whom were used to hard, rough riding. This was necessary, for when battle scenes are shown there must be some "killed," and when a man has a horse shot from under him, or is shot himself, riding at full speed, even though the cartridges are blank, the action calls for a heavy fall, sudden and abrupt, to make it look real. And this is not easy to do, nor is it altogether safe with a mob of riders thundering along behind one.

Yet the men who take part in these battle scenes do it with scarcely a thought of danger, though often many of them are hurt, as are the horses.

In brief the story of the play in which Ruth was to take the part of a girl in Blue, and Alice of a girl in Gray, was this. They were cousins, and Ruth was visiting Alice's home in the South when the war broke out. Alice, of course, sided with her people, and loved the gray uniforms, while Ruth's sympathies were with the North.

Ruth determined to go back North and become a nurse, while Alice, longing for more active work, offered her services as a spy to help the Confederacy. Though on opposite sides, the girls' love for one another did not wane.

Then came the scenes of the war. Battles were to be shown, and there were plots and counter-plots, in some of which Ruth and Alice had no part. Mr. DeVere was cast for a Northern General, and the character became him well. Later on Alice and Ruth were to meet in a hospital among the wounded. Alice was supposed to get certain papers of value to her side from a wounded Union officer. As she was escaping with them Ruth was to intercept her, and the two were to have a "strong" scene together.

Alice, ignoring the pleadings of her cousin and about to depart with the papers, learns that the officer from whom she took them was the same one that had saved her father's life on the battlefield. She decides to forego her mission as a spy, even though it may mean the betrayal of her own cause, when the news comes in of Lee's surrender, and her sacrifice is not demanded. Then "all live happily for ever after."

That is but a mere outline of the play, which was to be an elaborate production. And it was the rehearsal for the preliminary battles and skirmishes that the girls were now witnessing.

"Tell that battery to get ready to fire!" cried Mr. Pertell, and this word went over the telephone.

"Come on now with that Union charge!" was the next command.

Then hundreds of horses thundered down the slopes of Oak Farm, while the hidden guns thundered. Down went horses and men while the girls screamed involuntarily, it all seemed so real.

"It's a good thing we didn't plant no corn in that there field this season," observed Belix Apgar, Sandy's father, as he saw the charge.

"That's right," agreed his wife. "There wouldn't have been 'nuff left to make a hominy cake."

Laura Lee Hope

"Do it over again!" ordered the manager. "Some of you fellows ride your horses as if you were going to a croquet game. Get some action into it!"

Once more the battery thundered its harmless shots and the men charged. This time the scene was satisfactory, and preparations were made to film it. Again the men thundered down the slope, and when they were almost at the battery a single rider—a girl—dashed out toward the approaching Union soldiers.

"Oh, she'll be killed!" cried Ruth. "They'll ride right over her!"

It did seem so, for she was headed straight toward the approaching horsemen.

"She's all right," said Paul. "She's quite a rider, I believe. Her part, as a Union sympathizer, is to rush out and warn them of the hidden battery, but she is delayed by a Southerner until it is too late, and she takes a desperate chance. There go the guns!"

Horses and riders were lost in a cloud of smoke. This time the film was being taken. When that charge was over, and men and horses, some limping, had gone back to their quarters, Mr. Pertell signaled to the daring woman rider to come to him.

"That was very well done, Miss Brown," he said. "You certainly showed nerve."

"I am glad you liked it," was the answer in a quiet, well-bred voice. "Shall you want me again to-day?"

"Not until later, and it will be an interior. Is your horse

all right?"

"Oh, yes. I am in love with him!" and she patted the arching neck of the handsome creature. "He is so speedy."

"He sure is speedy, all right," agreed Paul, and the girl—she was scarcely more than that—who had been addressed as Miss Brown by the director smiled at the young actor. Then she let her friendly gaze rest on Ruth and Alice.

"Isn't she fine!" murmured Alice.

"Like to meet her?" whispered Paul.

"Yes!" exclaimed Alice eagerly, paying no attention to Ruth's plucking of her sleeve.

"Miss Brown, allow me to present—" and Paul introduced the two DeVere girls.

"That was a daring ride of yours!" remarked Alice, with enthusiasm.

"Indeed it was," agreed Ruth, more quietly.

"Do you think so? I'm glad you like it. I have been riding ever since I was a little girl."

"Did you learn in the West?" asked Alice.

"Why, yes—that is I—I really—oh, there goes that wild black horse again!" and Miss Brown turned to point to an animal ridden by one of the Confederate soldiers. The horse seemed unmanageable, and dashed some distance across the field before it was brought under control.

Then the talk turned to moving picture work, though Ruth could not help wondering, even in the midst of it, why Miss Brown had not been more certain of where she had learned to ride.

"It isn't something one would forget," mused Ruth.

CHAPTER VI

A NEEDED LESSON

Rehearsals, the filming of scenes, retakes and the studying of their parts kept busy not only the moving picture girls, but all the members of Mr. Pertell's company. There was work for all, and from the smallest girls and boys, including Tommie and Nellie Maguire, to Mr. DeVere himself, little spare time was to be had.

Ruth and Alice had important parts, and they were given a general outline of what was expected of them. They would be in many scenes, and a variety of action would be required. In order that they do themselves and the film justice, since they were to be "featured," the girls spent much time studying in their rooms and practising to get the best results from the various registerings.

"That is going to be a very strong scene for you and Alice," said Mr. DeVere to Ruth one day. "I refer to that scene where Alice takes the paper and afterwards discovers the identity of the man to whom she owes so much—the life of her father. Now let me see how you would play it, Alice."

Alice did so, and she did well, but her father was not satisfied. The stage traditions meant much to him, and though he had been forced to give up many of them when he went into the motion pictures, still he knew what good dramatic action was, and he knew that it would "get over" just as certainly in the silent drama as it did in the legitimate. So he made Alice go over the scene again, and Ruth also, until he was satisfied.

"Now, when the time comes, you'll know how to do it," he said. "Don't be satisfied with anything but the best you can do, even if it is only a moving picture show. I am convinced, more and more, that the silent drama is going to take a larger place than ever before the public."

It was on one afternoon following a rather hard day's work before the cameras, that Ruth and Alice, with Miss Pennington and Miss Dixon, sat on the porch of the farmhouse, waiting for the supper bell. Russ and Paul were off to one side, talking, and Mr. DeVere and Mr. Bunn were discussing their early days in the legitimate. Mr. Pertell came up the walk, a worried look on his face, seeing which Mr. Switzer called out:

"Did a cow step on some of the actors, Herr Director, or did one of our worthy farmer's rams knock over a camera after it had filmed one of the battle scenes?"

"Neither one, Mr. Switzer," was the answer. "This is merely a domestic trouble I have on my mind."

"Domestic!" exclaimed Alice. "You don't mean that some of your pretty extra girls have eloped with some of your dashing cowboy soldiers, do you? I wouldn't blame them if they—"

"Alice!" chided her sister.

"Oh, well, you know what I mean!"

"No, it isn't quite that," laughed the director, "though you have very nearly hit it," and he took a chair near Alice and her sister, and near where Pearl Pennington and Laura Dixon were rocking and chewing gum.

"Tell us, and perhaps we can help you," Alice suggested.

"Well, maybe you can. It's about Miss Estelle Brown, the young lady who made that daring ride in front of the masked battery the other day."

"What! Has she left?" asked Ruth. "She was such a wonderful rider!"

"No, she hasn't left, but she threatens to; and I can't let her go, as she's in some of the films and I'd have to switch the whole plot around to explain why she didn't come in on the later scenes."

"Why is she going to leave?" Alice queried.

"Because she has been subjected to some annoyance on the part of a young man who is one of the extras. You know the extras all live down in the big bungalow I had built for them. I have a man and his wife to look after them, and I try to make it as nearly like a happy family as I can. But Miss Brown says she can't stay there any longer. This young man—a decent enough chap he had seemed to me—is pestering her with his attentions. He is quite in love with her, it seems."

"Oh, how romantic!" gurgled Miss Dixon.

"Miss Brown doesn't think so," said the manager dryly. "I

Laura Lee Hope

don't know what to do about it, for I have no place where I can put her up alone."

"Bring her here!" exclaimed Alice, impulsively.

"Indeed, no!" cried Miss Pennington. "We actresses were told that none of the extra people would be quartered with us! If that had not been agreed to I would not have come to this place."

"Nor I!" chimed in Miss Dixon. "We professionals are not to be classed with these extras—and amateurs at that!"

"I know I did promise you regulars that you would be boarded by yourselves," said Mr. Pertell, scratching his head in perplexity, "and I don't blame you for not wanting, as a general run, to mix with the others. For some of them, while they are decent enough, have a big idea of their own importance. I wouldn't think of asking you to let one of the extra men come here, but this young lady—"

"She is perfectly charming!" broke in Alice. "And she certainly can ride!"

"She did seem very nice," murmured Ruth.

"Pooh! A vulgar cowgirl!" sneered Miss Dixon.

"There is a nice room near mine," went on Alice. "She could have that, I should think. The Apgars don't use it, and it is certainly annoying to be pestered by a young man!" and she looked with uptilted nose at Paul, who said emphatically:

"Well, I like that!"

"If I could bring her here—" began Mr. Pertell.

"By all means!" exclaimed Ruth. "We will try to make her happy and comfortable—if she is an amateur."

"She has no right to come here!" burst out Miss Dixon.

"No, indeed!" added Miss Pennington. "If she comes, I shall go! I will not board in the same place with an amateur cowgirl doing an extra turn in the pictures."

"Nor I!" snapped Miss Dixon.

"All right—all right!" said Mr. Pertell quickly. "I know it's contrary to my promise, and I won't insist on it. Only it would have made it easier—"

"Let Miss Brown come," quickly whispered Alice in the director's ear. "They won't leave. They're too comfortable here, and they get too good salaries. Let Miss Brown come!"

"Will you stand by me if I do?"

"Yes," said Alice.

"So will I," added Ruth.

Then the supper bell rang and the discussion ended for the time being. Later Mr. Pertell explained privately to Ruth and her sister that Miss Brown was a quiet and refined young lady about whom he knew little save that she had answered his advertisement for an amateur who could ride. She had made good and he had engaged her for the war scenes.

"But she tells me that among the young men in the same boarding bungalow is one who seems quite smitten with her. He is impudent and exceedingly persistent, and she does not desire his attentions. She said she thought she would have to

Laura Lee Hope

leave unless she could get a quiet place where he could not follow. It is all right during the day, as he can not come near her, but after hours—"

"Do bring her!" urged Alice. "We'll try to make her comfortable. And don't fear what they will do," and she nodded toward the two other actresses, who had been in vaudeville before going into motion pictures.

So it was that, later in the evening, Miss Brown brought her trunk to the Apgar farmhouse and was installed in a room near Alice and Ruth.

"Oh, it is *so* much nicer here!" sighed Estelle Brown, as she admitted Ruth and Alice, who knocked on her door. "I could not have stood the other place much longer. Though every one—except that one man—was very nice to me."

"Let us be your friends!" urged Alice.

"You are very kind," murmured Estelle, and the more the two girls looked at her, the prettier they thought her. She had wonderful hair, a marvelous complexion, and white, even teeth that made her smile a delight.

"Have you been in this business long?" asked Ruth.

"No, not very—in fact, this is my first big play. I have done little ones, but I did not get on very well. I love the work, though."

"Were your people in the profession?" asked Alice.

"I don't know—that is, I'm not sure. I believe some of them were, generations back. Oh, did you hear that?" and she interrupted her reply with the question.

"That" was the voice of some one in the lower hall inquiring if Miss Brown was in.

"It's that—that impertinent Maurice Whitlow!" whispered Estelle to Ruth and Alice. "I thought I could escape him here. Oh, what shall I do?"

"I'll say you are not at home," returned Ruth, in her best "stage society" manner, and, sweeping down the hall, she met the maid who was coming up to tell Miss Brown there was a caller for her below.

"Tell him Miss Brown is not at home," said Ruth.

"Very well," and the maid smiled understandingly.

"Ah! not at home? Tell her I shall call again," came in drawling tones up the stairway, for it was warm, and doors and windows were open.

"Little—snip!" murmured Estelle. "I'm so glad I didn't have to see him. He's a pest—all the while wanting to take me out and buy ice-cream sodas. He's just starting in at the movies, and he thinks he's a star already. Oh! but don't you just love the guns and horses?" she asked impulsively.

"Well, I can't say that I do," answered Ruth. "I like quieter plays."

"I don't!" cried Alice. "The more excitement the better I like it. I can do my best then."

"So can I," said Estelle. Then they fell to talking of the work, and of many other topics.

"Did Estelle Brown strike you as being peculiar?" asked

Ruth of her sister when they were back in their rooms, getting ready for bed.

"Peculiar? What do you mean?"

"I mean she didn't seem to know whether or not her people were in the profession."

"Yes, she did side-step that a bit."

"Side-step, Alice?"

"Well, avoid answering, if you like that better. But my way is shorter. Say, maybe she has gone into this without her people knowing it, and she wants to keep them from bringing her back."

"Maybe, though it didn't strike me as being that way. It was as though she wasn't quite sure of herself."

"Sure of herself—what do you mean?"

"Well, I can't explain it any better."

"I'll think it over," said Alice, sleepily. "We've got lots to do to-morrow," and she tumbled into bed with a drowsy "good-night."

Miss Laura Dixon and Miss Pearl Pennington most decidedly turned up their noses at the breakfast table when they saw Estelle sitting between Ruth and Alice. And their murmurs of disdain could be plainly heard.

"She here? Then I'm going to leave!"

"The idea of amateurs butting in like this! It's a shame!"

Fortunately Estelle was exchanging some gay banter with Paul and did not hear. But Ruth and Alice did, and the latter could not avoid a thrust at the scornful ones. To Ruth, in an unnecessarily loud voice, Alice remarked:

"Do you remember that funny vaudeville stunt we used to laugh over when we were children—'The Lady Bookseller?'"

"Yes, I remember it very well," answered Ruth. "What about it, Alice?" for she did not catch her sister's drift.

"Why, I was just wondering how many years ago it was—ten, at least, since it was popular, isn't it?"

"I believe so!"

"It's no such a thing!" came the indignant remonstrance from Miss Pennington. It was in this sketch that she had made her "hit," and as she now claimed several years less than the number to which she was entitled, this sly reference to her age was not relished. "It was only *six* years ago that I starred in that," she went on.

"It seems much longer," said Alice, calmly. "We were quite little when we saw you in that. You were so funny with your big feet—"

"Big feet! I had to wear shoes several sizes too large for me! It was in the act. I—I—"

"They're stringing you—keep still!" whispered her chum, and with red cheeks Miss Pennington subsided.

But Alice's remarks had the desired effect, and there were no more references, for the present, directed at pretty Estelle. Miss Dixon and Miss Pennington had a scene with Mr.

Laura Lee Hope

Pertell, though, in which they threatened to leave unless Estelle were sent back to the bungalow where the other extra players boarded. But the manager remained firm, and the two vaudeville actresses did not quit the company.

Hard work followed, and Estelle made some daring rides, once narrowly escaping injury from the burning wad of a cannon, which went off prematurely as she dashed past the very muzzle. But she put spurs to her horse, who leaped over the spurt of fire and smoke. A few feet of film were spoiled; but this was better than having an actor hurt.

Alice was sitting on the farmhouse porch one afternoon, waiting for Estelle and Ruth to come down, for they were going for a walk together, not being needed in the films. Estelle had been taken into companionship by the two girls, who found her a very charming companion, though little disposed to talk about herself.

Alice, who was reading a motion picture magazine, was startled by hearing a voice saying, almost in her ear:

"Is Miss Brown in?"

"Oh!" and Alice looked up to see Maurice Whitlow smirking at her. He had tiptoed up on the porch and was standing very close to her. She had never been introduced to him, but that is not absolutely insisted on in moving picture circles, particularly when a company is on "location."

"Is Miss Brown in?" repeated Whitlow.

"I don't know, I'm sure," replied Alice.

"Ah, well, I'll wait and find out. I'll sit down here by you and wait," went on the young man, drawing a chair so close to that of Alice that it touched. "Fine day, isn't it? I say! you did that bit of acting very cleverly to-day."

"Did I?" and Alice went on reading.

"Yes. I had a little bit myself. I carried a message from the field headquarters to the rear—after more ammunition, you know. Did you notice me riding?"

"I did not."

"Well, I saw you, all right. If Miss Brown isn't home, do you want to go over to the village with me?"

"I do not!" and Alice was very emphatic.

"Then for a row on the lake?"

"No!"

"You look as though you would enjoy canoeing," went on the persistent Whitlow. "You have a very strong little hand—very pretty!" and he boldly reached up and removed Alice's fingers from the edge of the magazine. "A very pretty little hand—yes!" and he sighed foolishly.

"How dare you!" cried Alice, indignantly. "If you don't—"

"See how you like that pretty bit of grass down there!" exclaimed a sharp voice behind Alice, and the next moment Mr. Maurice Whitlow, eye-glasses, lavender tie, socks and all, went sailing over the porch railing, to land in a sprawling heap on the sod below.

CHAPTER VII

ESTELLE'S LEAP

"Oh!" murmured Alice, shrinking down in her chair. "Oh—my!"

She gave a hasty glance over her shoulder, to behold Paul Ardite standing back of her chair, an angry look on his face. Then Alice looked at the sprawling form of the extra player. He was getting up with a dazed expression on his countenance.

"What—what does this mean?" he gasped, striving to make his tones indignant. But it is hard for dignity to assert itself when one is on one's hands and knees in the grass, conscious that there is a big grass stain on one's white cuff, and with one's clothing generally disarranged. "What does this mean? I demand an explanation," came from Mr. Maurice Whitlow.

"You know well enough what it means!" snapped Paul. "If you don't, why, come back here and try it over again and I'll give you another demonstration!"

"Oh, don't, Paul—please!" pleaded Alice in a low voice.

"There's no danger. He won't come," was the confident reply.

By this time Whitlow had picked himself up and was brushing his garments. He settled his collar, straightened his lavender tie and wet his lips as though about to speak.

"You—you—I—" he began. "I don't see what right you had to—"

"That'll do now!" interrupted Paul, sternly. "It's of no use to go into explanations. You know as well as I do what you were doing and why I pitched you over the railing. I'll do it again if you want me to, but twice as hard. And if I catch you here again, annoying any of the ladies of this company, I'll report you to the director. Now skip—and stay skipped!" concluded Paul significantly. "Perhaps you can't read that notice?" and he pointed to one recently posted on the main gateway leading to the big farmhouse. It was to the effect that none of the extra players were allowed admission to the grounds without a permit from the director.

"Huh! I'm as good an actor as you, any day!" sneered Whitlow, as he limped down the walk.

"Maybe. But you can't get over with it—here!" said Paul significantly.

The notice had been posted because so many of the cowboys and girls had fairly overrun the precincts of Mr. Apgar's home. He and his family had no privacy at all, and while they did not mind the regular members of Mr. Pertell's company, with whom they were acquainted, they did not want the hundreds of extra men, soldiers, cowboys and horsewomen running all over the place.

So the rule had been adopted, and it was observed good-naturedly by those to whom it applied. Whitlow must have considered himself above it.

"Did he annoy you much, Alice?" asked Paul.

"Not so very. He was just what you might call—fresh. He asked for Miss Brown, and when she wasn't here to snub him he turned the task over to me. Ugh!" and Alice began to scrub vigorously with her handkerchief the fingers which Whitlow had grasped. "I'm sorry you had that trouble with him, Paul," she went on. "But really—"

"It was no trouble—it was a pleasure!" laughed Paul. "I'd like to do it over again if it were not for annoying you. I happened to come up behind and heard what he was saying. So I just pitched into him. I don't believe he'll come back. He'll be too much afraid of losing the work. Mr. Pertell has had a great many applications from players out of work who want to be taken on as extras, and he can have his pick. So those that don't obey the regulations will get short notice. You won't be troubled with him again."

And Alice was not, nor was Miss Brown. That is, as regards the extra player's trespassing on the grounds about the farmhouse. But he was of the kind that is persistent, and on several occasions, when the duties of the girls brought them near to where Whitlow was acting, he smiled and smirked at them.

Alice wished to tell Paul about it and have him administer another and more severe chastisement to Whitlow, but Ruth and Estelle persuaded the impulsive one to forego doing so.

"I can look after myself, thank you, Alice dear," Estelle said. "Now that I don't have to board in the bungalow with him it is easier."

"Don't make a scene," advised Ruth.

"Oh, but I just can't bear to have him look at me," Alice said.

Several of the scenes in the principal drama had been made, but most of the largest ones, those of the battles, of Alice's spy work, and of Ruth's nursing, were yet to come.

The making of a big moving picture is the work not of days, but of weeks, and often of months. If every scene took place in a studio, where artificial lights could be used, the filming could go on every day the actors were on hand, or whenever the director felt like working them and the camera men. Often in a studio, even, the director will be notional—"temperamental," he might call it—and let a day go by, and again the glare of the powerful lights may so affect the eyes of the players that they have to rest, and so time is lost in that way.

But the time lost in a studio is as nothing compared to the time lost in filming the big outdoor scenes. There the sun is a big factor, for a brilliant light is needed to take pictures of galloping horses, swiftly moving automobiles and loco-motives, and every cloudy day means a loss of time. For this reason many of the big film companies maintain studios in California, where there are many days of sunshine. They can take "outdoor stuff" almost any time after the sun is up.

But at Oak Farm there were times when everything would be in readiness for a big scene, the camera men waiting, the players ready to dash into their parts, and then clouds would form, or it would rain, and there would be a postponement. But it was part of the game, and as the salaries of the players went on whether they worked or not, they did not complain.

One morning Alice, on going into Estelle's room, found her busy "padding" herself before she put on her outer garments.

"What in the world are you doing?" Alice asked.

"Getting ready for my big jump," was the answer.

"Your big jump?"

"Yes, you know there is a scene where I carry a message from headquarters to one of the Union generals at the front. Your father plays the latter part."

"Oh, yes, now I remember. And Daddy is sure no one can do quite as well as he can in the tent scene, where he salutes you and takes the message you have brought through with such peril."

"Yes, that's nice. Well, I'm to ride along and be pursued by some Confederate guerrillas. It's a race, and I decide to take a short cut, not knowing the Confederates have burned the bridge. I have to leap my horse down an embankment and ford the stream. I'm getting ready for the jump now—that's why I'm padding myself. For Petro—that's my horse—might slip or stumble in jumping down that embankment, and I want to be ready to roll out of the way. It's much more comfortable to roll in a padded suit—like a football player's—than in your ordinary clothes. Your friend, Russ Dalwood, told me to do this, and I think it is a good idea."

"It's sure to be if Russ told you, isn't it, Ruth?" asked Alice, with a mischievous look at her sister, who had just come in.

"How should I know?" was the cool response. "I suppose Mr. Dalwood knows what he is doing, though."

"Oh, how very formal we are all of a sudden," mocked Alice. "You two haven't quarreled, have you?"

"Silly," returned Ruth, blushing.

"Are you really going to jump your horse down a cliff?" asked Alice.

"I really am," was the smiling answer. "There is to be no fake about this. But really there is little danger. I am so used to horses."

"Yes, and I marvel at you," put in Ruth. "Where did you learn it all?"

"I don't know. It seems to come natural to me."

"You must have lived on a ranch a long time," ventured Ruth.

"Did I? Well, perhaps I did. Say, lace this up the back for me, that's a dear," and she turned around so that Alice or Ruth could fasten a corset-like pad that covered a large part of her body. It would not show under her dress, but would be a protection in case of a fall.

Alice and Ruth were so greatly interested in the coming perilous leap of Estelle's that they did not pursue their inquiries about her life on a ranch, though Alice casually remarked that it was strange she did not speak more about it.

The two DeVere girls had no part in this one scene, and they went to watch it, safely out of range of the cameras. For there were to be two snapping this jump, to avoid the necessity of a retake in case one film failed.

"All ready now!" called Mr. Pertell, when there had been several rehearsals up to the actual point of making the jump. Estelle had raced out of the woods bearing the message. The

Confederate guerrillas had pursued her, and she had found the bridge burned—one built for the purpose and set fire to.

"All ready for the jump?" asked the director.

"All ready," Estelle answered, looking to saddle girths and stirrups.

"Then come on!" yelled the director through his megaphone.

Estelle urged her horse forward. With shouts and yells, which, of course, had no part in the picture, yet which served to aid them in their acting, the players who were portraying the Confederates came after her, spurring their horses and firing wildly. On and on rushed the steed bearing the daring girl rider.

She reached the place of the burned bridge, halted a moment, made a gesture of despair, and then raced for the bank, down which she would leap her horse to the ford.

"Come on! Come on!" yelled Mr. Pertell. "That's fine! Come on! You men there put a little more pep in your riding. Turn and fire at them, Miss Brown! Fire one shot, and one of you men reel in his saddle. That's the idea!"

Estelle had quickly turned and fired, and one man had most realistically showed that he was hit, afterward slumping from his seat.

Now the girl was at the edge of the bank. She was to make a flying jump over its edge and come down in the soft sand, sliding to the bottom—in the saddle if she could keep her seat, rolling over and over if, perchance, she left it.

"That's the idea! Get every bit of that, Russ! That's fine!"

yelled Mr. Pertell.

"There she goes!" cried Alice, grasping her sister's arm, and as she spoke Estelle spurred her horse and it leaped full and fair over the edge of the embankment. Estelle had made her big jump. Would she come safely out of it?

Laura Lee Hope

CHAPTER VIII

A MASSED ATTACK

While Russ Dalwood and his helper were grinding their cameras, reeling away at the film on which was being impressed the shifting vision of Estelle Brown taking her hazardous leap, Alice, Ruth, and the others were watching to see how the daring young horsewoman would come out of it.

"She's going to land in a minute!" exclaimed Miss Dixon.

"In a minute? In a half second!" cried Alice. "But don't talk!"

"There—she's fallen!" gasped Miss Pennington.

With his feet gathered under him, Petro had come down straight on the sliding, shifting sand of the embankment. For a moment it looked as though he had stumbled and that Estelle would be thrown.

But she held a firm rein, and leaned far back in the saddle. The horse stiffened and then, keeping upright with his forelegs straight out in front of him and his hind ones bunched under him, he began to slide.

Down the embankment he slid, as the Italian cavalrymen

sometimes ride their horses, with Estelle firm in the saddle. And, as a matter of fact, the girl said afterward it was from having seen some moving pictures of these Italian army riders that she got the idea of doing as she did.

"She won't fall!" murmured Paul.

"Oh, I'm so glad! The picture will be a success, won't it?"

"I should think so," Paul said. "It certainly was a daring ride."

"I wouldn't mind doing it if I had her horse," put in Maurice Whitlow, smirking at the girls. "I think you could do that, Miss DeVere," and he looked at Alice.

She turned away with only a murmured reply, but, nothing daunted, the "pest" went on:

"Estelle is certainly a fine rider. I think she must have been a cowgirl on a ranch at one time, though she won't admit it."

"She wouldn't to you, at any rate," said Paul, significantly.

"Why not?"

"Oh, if you don't know it's of no use to tell you. Look! Now she goes into the water!"

The action called for the halting at the top of the embankment of the Confederate riders, who dared not make the jump. They fired some futile shots at Estelle, then rode around to a less dangerous descent to try to catch her. But Estelle was to ford the stream and continue on to the Union lines with her message.

Reaching the bottom of the slope, her horse gathered himself together for another bit of moving picture work. At the edge of the stream another camera man was stationed, for Estelle and her horse were by this time too far away from Russ and his helper to make good views possible.

Into the water splashed the girl, urging on her spirited horse, that was none the worse for his jump and his long slide.

"Good work! Good work!" cried an assistant director, who was stationed near the stream to see that all went according to the scenario. "Keep on, Miss Brown!"

Estelle bent low over her horse's neck, to escape possible bullets from the Confederate guns, and on and on she raced until she pulled up at the tent of "General" DeVere. Here her mission ended, after the father of Alice and Ruth, in a dusty uniform of a Union officer, had come out in response to the summons from his orderly.

Estelle slipped from her saddle, registered exhaustion, saluted and held out the paper she had brought through the Confederate lines at such risk. Nor was the risk wholly one of the play, for she might have been seriously hurt in her perilous leap.

But, fortunately, everything came out properly and a fine series of pictures resulted.

"I'm so glad!" Estelle exclaimed, when it was all over, and, divested of her padding, she sat in her room with Ruth and Alice. "I want to 'make good' in this business, and riding seems to be my forte."

"Do you like it better than anything else?" asked Alice.

"Yes, I do. And I just love moving pictures, don't you?"

"Indeed we do," put in Ruth. "But we were never cut out for riders."

"I'd like it!" exclaimed Alice. "I'd like to know how to ride a horse as well as you do."

"I'll show you," offered Estelle. "I'll be very glad to, and it's easy. It's like swimming—all you need is confidence, and to learn not to be afraid of your horse but to trust him. Let me show you some day."

"I believe I will!" decided Alice, with flashing eyes. "It will be great."

"Better ask father," suggested Ruth.

"Oh, he'll let me, I know. We've ridden some, you know; but I would like to ride as well as Estelle," and Alice and Estelle began to talk over their plans for taking and giving riding lessons. In the midst of the talk the return of the boy who went daily to the village for mail was announced.

"Oh, I hope my new waist has come!" Alice exclaimed, for she had written to her dressmaker to send one by parcel post. There was a package for her—the one she expected—and also some letters, as well as one for Ruth. Estelle showed no interest when the distribution of the mail was going on.

"Don't you expect anything?" asked Alice.

"Any what?"

"Letters."

Laura Lee Hope

"Why, no, I don't believe I do," was the slowly given answer. "I don't write any, so I don't get any, I suppose," and both girls noticed that there was a far-away look in Estelle's eyes. Perhaps it was a wistful look, for surely all girls like to get letters from some one.

"I believe she is estranged from her family," decided Alice to her sister afterward. "Did you see how pathetic she looked when we got letters and she didn't?"

"Well, I didn't notice anything special," Ruth replied. "But there is something queer about her, I must admit. She is so absent-minded at times. This morning I asked her if she wanted to go for a walk, and she said she had no ticket."

"No ticket?"

"Yes, that's what she said. And when I laughed and told her one didn't need a ticket to walk around Oak Farm, she sort of 'came to' and said she was thinking about a boat."

"A boat—what boat?"

"That was all she said. Then she began to talk about something else."

"Do you know what I think?" asked Alice, suddenly.

"No. But then you think so many things it isn't any wonder I can't keep track of them."

"I think, as I believe I've said before, that she has run away from some ranch to be in moving pictures. That's why she doesn't write or receive letters. She doesn't want her folks to know where she is."

"I can hardly believe that," declared Ruth. "She is too nice and refined a girl to have done anything like that. No, I just think she is a bit queer, that is all. But certainly she doesn't tell much about herself."

However, further speculation regarding Estelle Brown was cut short, as orders came for the appearance of nearly the entire company in one of the plays.

The first scene was to take place in a Southern town, and for the purpose a street had been constructed by Pop Snooks and his helpers. There was a stately mansion, smaller houses, a store or two and some other buildings. True, the buildings were but shells, and, in some cases, only fronts, but they showed well in the picture.

Ruth, Alice, and a number of the girls and women and men were to be the inhabitants of this village, and were to take part in an alarm and flee the place when it was known that the Confederate forces were being driven back and through the place by the Unionists.

"Come on—get dressed!" cried Alice, and soon she, her sister, Estelle and the other women were donning their Southern costumes, wide skirts, with hoops to puff them out, and broad-brimmed hats, under which curls showed.

There was to be a massed attack by the Unionists on the town, through which the Confederates were to flee, and it was the part of Ruth and Alice to rush from their father's "mansion" bearing a few of their choice possessions.

All was in readiness. The Southern defenders were on the outskirts of the town, drawn up to receive the Unionists. Toward these Confederates, their enemies came riding. This was filmed separately, while other camera men, in the made street, took pictures of the activities there. Men, women and children went in and out of the houses. Though, as Mr. Belix Apgar said, "If you call them houses you might as well call the smell of an onion a dinner. There ain't nothin' to 'em!"

Suddenly an excited rider dashed into the midst of the peaceful activities of the Southern town.

"They're coming! They're coming!" he cried, waving his hat. "The Yankees are coming!" This would be flashed on the screen.

Then ensued a wild scene. Colored mammies rushed here and there seeking their charges. Men began to look to their arms. Then came the advance guard of the retreating Confederates, turning back to fire at their enemies.

"Come on now, Ruth—Alice! This is where we make our rush—just as the first of the Union soldiers appear!" called Paul, who was acting the part of a Southern youth. "Grab up your stuff and come on!"

Ruth was to carry a bandbox and a case supposed to contain the family jewels. Alice, who played the part this time of a frivolous young woman, was to save her pet cat.

"Here they come!" yelled Paul, as the first of the Unionists came into view at the head of the street. "Hurry, girls!"

Out they rushed, down the steps of the mansion, fleeing before the mounted Union soldiers, who laughed and jeered, firing at the Confederates, who were retreating.

Ruth and Estelle, with some of the other women, were in the lead. Alice had lingered behind, for the cat showed a disposition to wiggle out of her arms, and she wanted to keep it to make an effective picture.

Finally the creature did make its escape, but Alice was not going to give up so easily. She started in pursuit, and then one of the Union soldiers, Maurice Whitlow, spurred his horse forward. He wanted to get in the foreground of the picture and took this chance.

"Get back where you belong!" yelled the director angrily. "Who told you to get in the spotlight? Get back!"

But it was too late. Alice, in pursuit of the cat, was running straight toward Whitlow's horse, and the next moment she slipped and went down, almost under the feet of the prancing animal.

Laura Lee Hope

CHAPTER IX

MISS DIXON'S LOSS

"Look out!" shouted Paul, and, dropping what he was carrying, he made a leap toward the animal Whitlow was riding.

"Roll out of the way of his feet!" cried the director.

"Shall I keep on with the film?" asked the camera man, for his duty was to turn until told to stop, no matter what happened.

"Let it run!" Alice cried. "I can get out of the way. Don't stop on my account!"

She had been in motion pictures long enough to know what it meant to spoil a hundred feet or more of film in a spirited picture, necessitating a retake. She had seen her danger, and had done her best to get out of harm's way.

The cat had leaped into some bushes and was out of sight.

Whitlow, his face showing his fear and his inability to act in this emergency, had instinctively drawn back on the reins. But it was to the intelligent horse itself, rather than to the rider, that Alice owed her immunity from harm. For the horse reared, and came down with feet well to one side of the crouching girl, who had partly risen to her knees.

At the same moment Paul sprang for the steed's bridle and swerved him to one side. Then, seeing that Alice was practically out of danger, Paul's rage at the carelessness of Whitlow rose, and he reached up and fairly dragged that young man out of the saddle.

"You don't know enough to lead a horse to water, let alone ride one in a movie battle scene!" he cried, as he pushed the player to one side. "Why don't you look where you're going?"

Whitlow was too shaken and startled to reply.

"Go on. Help her up and keep on with the retreat!" cried the director. "That's one of the best scenes of the picture. Couldn't have been better if we had rehearsed it. Never mind the cat, Miss DeVere. Run on. Paul, you land a couple of blows on Whitlow and then follow Alice. Hold back, there—you Union men—until we get this bit of by-play."

Paul, nothing loath, gave Whitlow two hard blows, and the latter dared not return them for fear of spoiling the picture, but he muttered in rage.

Then Paul, shaking his fist at the Unionists, hurried on after Alice, and the retreat continued. What had threatened to be a disaster, or at least a spoiling of the scene, had turned out well. It is often so in moving pictures.

In the remainder of the scene the girls had little part. They had been driven from their home, and, presumably, were taken in by friends. The rest of the scenes showed the Union soldiers making merry in the Southern town they had captured.

"My! That was a narrow escape you had!" exclaimed Ruth, when she and her sister were at liberty to return to the farmhouse. "Were you hurt?"

"No; I strained one arm just a little. But it will make a good scene, so Russ said."

"Too good—too realistic!" declared Paul. "When I get a chance at that Whitlow—"

"Please don't do anything!" begged Alice. "It wasn't really his fault. If I hadn't had the cat—"

"It was his fault for pushing himself to the front the way he did," said the young actor. "Only the best riders were picked to lead the charge. He might have known he couldn't control his horse in an emergency. That's where he was at fault."

"He is a poor rider," commented Estelle. "But you showed rare good sense, Alice, in acting as you did. A horse will not step on a person if he can possibly avoid it. Mr. Whitlow's horse was better than he was."

"Just the same, I got in two good punches!" chuckled Paul, "and he didn't dare hit back."

"He may make trouble for you later," Alice said.

"Oh, I'm not worrying about that. I'm satisfied."

There was a spirited battle scene later in the day between the Union and Confederate forces; the latter endeavoring to retake the village.

A Confederate battery in a distant town was sent for, and the Union position was shelled. But as by this time the Union cannon had come up and were entrenched in the town, an artillery duel ensued.

Views were shown of the Union guns being manned by the men, who wore bloody cloths around their foreheads and who worked hard serving the cannon. Real powder was used, but no balls, of course, and now and then a man would fall dead at his gun.

Similar views with another camera were taken of the Confederate guns and the scenes alternated on the screen afterward, creating a big sensation.

Then came an attack of the Confederate infantry under cover of the Southern battery. This was spirited, detachments of men rushing forward, firing and then seeking what cover they could. At times a man would roll over, his gun dropping, sometimes several would drop at the same time. These were those who were detailed to be shot.

The Unionists replied with a counter charge, and for a time the battle waged fiercely on both sides. Then came a lull in the fighting, with the Confederates ready to make a last charge in a desperate attempt to recapture the town.

"I know what would make a good scene," said Maurice Whitlow, during the lull when fresh films were being loaded into the cameras. "If we had an airship now some of us Union fellows could go for reinforcements in that. It would make a dandy scene."

"An airship!" cried Russ. "Say! remember that these scenes are supposed to have taken place in 1863. The only airships then were those the inventors were dreaming about or making in their laboratories. No airships in Civil War plays! I guess not! Balloons, maybe, but no airships."

"More fighting! Camera!" called Mr. Pertell, and again the spirited action was under way. Cannon boomed; rifles spat fire and smoke; men fought hand to hand, often rolling over dead; riderless horses dashed here and there. Now and then a man would narrowly escape being run down. As it was, several were burned from being too near the cannon or the guns, and one man's leg was broken in a fall from his horse.

But it was part of the game, and no one seemed to mind. A real hospital was set up at Oak Farm, not a mere shell of a building, and here the injured, as well as those who simulated injury, were attended.

Ruth and some of the women made up as nurses, though this was not the big scene in which Ruth and Alice were to take part.

"Confederates retreat!" directed Mr. Pertell, and the Southern forces, having been defeated, were forced to withdraw. Their attempt to recapture their town had failed.

"Whew! that was hot work!" cried Paul, as he came back to the farmhouse, having played his part as a Confederate soldier.

"It certainly was," agreed Mr. DeVere, who had been the directing Union General. Now that the "war" was over Northerners and Southerners mingled together in friendly converse, their differences forgotten.

"I just can't bear the smell of powder!" complained Miss Dixon. "I wish I had my salts."

"I'll get them for you, dear," offered Miss Pennington. "I'm going up to our rooms." The former vaudeville actresses, with Ruth, Alice, and some of the others, were resting on the farmhouse porch.

Miss Dixon smelled the salts and declared she felt much better.

"There's to be a dance in the village to-night," Paul remarked at the supper table.

"Let's go!" proposed Alice. "Will you take me, Paul?"

"Of course I will."

"May I have the pleasure?" asked Russ, of Ruth.

"Why, yes, if the rest go."

"We'll all go!" chimed in Miss Dixon. "Some of the extra men are good dancers. They proved it in the ballroom scene the other day. We can get a man, Pearl."

"All right, my dear, just as you say."

The little party was soon arranged.

"Estelle might like to go," suggested Alice.

"I'll go to ask her," offered Ruth, for Miss Brown had quit the supper table early and gone to her room.

As Ruth mounted the stairs she heard Miss Dixon and Miss Pennington talking in the hall outside their rooms.

"I can't see where it can be," Miss Dixon was saying.

"It was on your dresser when I went up for the salts," said her chum. "Are you sure you didn't take it after that?"

"Positive! It's gone—that's all there is to it."

"What's gone?" asked Ruth.

"One of my rings," was Miss Dixon's answer. "I left it on my dresser and my door was open. It was there when I went down to supper, and we were all at the table together—"

"Except Estelle Brown!" said Miss Pennington quickly.

CHAPTER X

LIEUTENANT VARLEY

For a moment Ruth stood looking with wide-open eyes at the two former vaudeville actresses. On their part they stared boldly at Ruth, and then Miss Dixon turned and slightly winked at Miss Pennington.

"That was one of your valuable rings, wasn't it, dear?" asked Miss Pennington, in deliberate tones.

"It certainly was—the best diamond I had. I simply won't let it be lost—or taken. I'm going to have it back!"

She spoke in a loud tone, and the door of Estelle's room, farther down the hall, opened. Estelle looked out. She was in negligee, and she seemed to be suffering.

"Has anything happened?" she asked.

"Yes," answered Miss Dixon. "Something has happened. Some one has stolen my diamond ring!"

"Oh!" gasped Ruth, "you shouldn't say that!"

"Say what?"

Laura Lee Hope

"Stolen. It's such a—such a harsh word."

"Well, I feel harsh just now. I'm not going to lose that ring. It was on my dresser when I went down to supper, and now it's gone. It was stolen—or taken, if you like that word better. Perhaps you want me to say it was—borrowed?" and she looked scornfully at Ruth.

"It may have slipped down behind your dresser."

"I've looked," said Miss Pennington. "You came up here from the table before we did," she went on, addressing Estelle. "Did you see anything of any one in Miss Dixon's room?"

"I? No, I saw no one." Estelle was plainly taken by surprise.

"Did you go in yourself," asked Miss Dixon brusquely. "Come, I don't mind a joke—if it was a joke—but give me back my ring. I'm going into town, and I want to wear it."

"A joke! Give you back your ring! Why, what do you mean?" and Estelle, her face flashing her indignation, stepped out into the hall.

"I mean you might have borrowed it," went on Miss Dixon, not a whit daunted. "Oh, it isn't anything. I've often done the same thing myself when we've been playing on circuit. It's all right—if you give things back."

"But I haven't taken anything of yours!" cried Estelle. "I never went into your room!"

"Perhaps you have forgotten about it," suggested Miss Pennington coldly. "You seem to have a headache, and sometimes those headache remedies are so strong—"

"I am tired, but I have no headache," said Estelle simply, "nor have I taken any strong headache remedies, as you seem to suggest. I haven't been walking in my sleep, either. And I certainly was not in your room, Miss Dixon, nor do I know anything about your ring," and with that she turned and entered her room, whence, presently, came the sound of sobbing.

For a moment Ruth stood still, looking at the two rather flashy actresses, and wondering if they really meant what they had insinuated. Then Alice's voice was heard calling:

"I say, Ruth, are you and Estelle coming? The boys have the auto and they'll take us in. Come on."

Ruth did not answer, and Alice came running up the stairs. She came to a halt as she saw the trio standing in the hall.

"Well, for the love of trading stamps! what's it all about?" she asked. "Are you posing for Faith, Hope and Charity?"

"Certainly not Charity," murmured Ruth.

"And I certainly have lost what little faith I had, though I hope I do get my ring back," sneered Miss Dixon.

"Your ring? What's the matter?" asked Alice. "Have you lost something?"

"My diamond ring was taken off my dresser," said the actress.

"And that Estelle Brown was up here ahead of us, and all alone," said Miss Pennington. "She may have borrowed it and forgotten to return it."

"That's what one gets for leaving one's valuable diamond rings around where these extra players are allowed to have free access," sneered Miss Dixon.

"You mean that little chip diamond ring of yours with the red garnets around it?" asked Alice.

"It isn't a chip diamond at all!" fired back Miss Dixon. "It was a valuable ring."

"Comparatively, perhaps, yes," and Alice's voice was coolly sneering, though she rarely allowed herself this privilege. "I'm sorry it is lost—"

"Why don't you say taken?" asked Miss Pennington.

"Because I don't believe it was," snapped Alice. "Either you forgot where you laid it or it has dropped behind something. As for thinking Estelle Brown even borrowed it, that's all nonsense! I don't believe a word of it."

"Nor I!" exclaimed Ruth.

"Did you speak to her about it?" asked Alice, and then as the sound of sobbing came from Estelle's room she burst out with:

"You horrid things! I believe you did! Shame on you!" and she hurried to the closed door.

"It is I—Alice," she whispered. "Let me in. It's all a terrible mistake. Don't let it affect you so, Estelle dear!"

Then Alice opened the unlocked door and went in. Ruth paused for a moment to say:

"I think you have made a terrible mistake, Miss Dixon," and then she followed her sister to comfort the crying girl.

"Humph! Mistake!" sneered Miss Dixon.

"That's what we get for mixing in with amateurs," added her chum. "Come on, we'll speak to Mr. Pertell about it."

But, for some reason or other, the director was not told directly of the loss of the ring, nor was Estelle openly accused. She felt as badly, though, as if she had been, even when Ruth and Alice tried to comfort her.

Estelle had left the table early, but though she had passed Miss Dixon's room, she said she had seen no one about.

"Don't mind about the old ring!" said Alice. "It wasn't worth five dollars."

"But that I should be accused of taking even five dollars!"

"You're not!" said Ruth, quickly. "They don't dare make an open accusation. I wouldn't be surprised if Miss Dixon found she had lost her ring and she's ashamed to acknowledge it."

"Oh, but it is dreadful to be suspected!" sighed Estelle.

"You're not—no one in his senses would think of even dreaming you took so much as a pin!" cried Alice. "It's positively silly! I wouldn't make such a fuss over such a cheap ring."

But Miss Dixon did make a "fuss," inasmuch as she talked often about her loss, though she still made no direct accusation against Estelle. But Miss Dixon and her chum made life miserable for the daring horsewoman. They often spoke in her presence of extra players who did not know their places, and made sneering references to locking up their valuables.

At times Estelle was so miserable that she threatened to leave, but Ruth and Alice would not hear of it and offered to lay the whole matter before Mr. Pertell and have him settle it by demanding that the loser of the ring either make a direct accusation or else keep quiet about her loss.

Mr. DeVere, who was appealed to by his daughters, voted against this, however.

"It is best not to pay any attention to those young ladies," he advised. "The friends of Estelle know she would not do such a thing, and no one takes either Miss Dixon or Miss Pennington very seriously—not half as seriously as they take themselves. It will all blow over."

There were big times ahead for the moving picture girls and their friends. Some of the most important battle scenes were soon to be filmed, those that had already been taken having been skirmishes.

"I have succeeded in getting two regiments of the state militia to take part in a sham battle for our big play," said Mr. Pertell one day. "They are to come to this part of the country for their annual manoeuvers under the supervision of the regular army officers, and by paying their expenses I can have them here for a couple of days.

"They will come with their horses, tents, and everything, so we shall have some real war scenes—that is, as real as can be had with blank cartridges. It will be a great thing for my film."

"And will they work in with our players?" asked Mr. DeVere.

"Oh, yes, indeed! I intend to use your daughters in the spy and hospital scenes, and you as one of the generals. In fact, Mr. DeVere, I depend on you to coach the militia men. For though they know a lot about military matters, they do not know how best to pose for the camera. So I'll be glad if you will act as a sort of stage manager."

"I shall be pleased to," answered the old player. And he was greatly delighted at the opportunity.

About a week after Mr. Pertell had mentioned that two regiments of militia were coming to Oak Farm, Ruth and Alice awakened one morning to see the fields about them dotted with tents and soldiers moving about here and there.

"Why, it does look just like a real war camp!" exclaimed Alice, who, in a very becoming dressing gown, was at the window. "Oh, isn't it thrilling! How dare you?" she exclaimed, drawing hastily back.

"What was it?" asked Ruth from her room.

"One of the officers had the audacity to wave his hand at me."

"You shouldn't have looked out."

"Ha! A pity I can't look out of my own window," and to prove that she was well within her rights Alice looked out again, and pretended not to see a young man who was standing in the yard below.

There was a bustle of excitement at the breakfast table. All

Laura Lee Hope

the players were eager to know what parts they would have, for this was the biggest thing any of them had yet been in—with two regiments taking the field one against the other, with many more cannon and guns than Mr. Pertell had hitherto used.

"I'll be able to throw on the screen a real battle scene," he said.

"The only trouble," declared Pop Snooks, "is that their uniforms aren't like those of the days of sixty-three." Pop was a stickler for dramatic correctness.

"It won't matter," said Mr. Pertell. "The views of the battle will be distant ones, and no one will be able to see the kind of uniforms the men wear. Those who are close to the camera will wear the proper Civil War uniforms we have on hand. The officers of the Guard have agreed to that."

Considerable preparation was necessary before the big film of the battle could be taken, and to this end it was necessary to have several conferences among the officers and Mr. Pertell and his camera men and assistants, including Mr. DeVere. A number of the Guard officers were constantly about the farmhouse, arranging the plans.

One afternoon Alice was sitting on the porch with Estelle, waiting until it was time for them to take their parts in a side scene of the production. A nattily attired young officer came up the walk, doffing his cap.

"I beg your pardon," he said. "I am Lieutenant Varley, and I was sent here to ask for Mr. Pertell. Perhaps you can tell me where I can find him?"

Alice looked and blushed. He was the one who had

audaciously waved to her beneath her window, but now he showed no sign of recognition. As his gaze rested on the face of Estelle Brown, however, he started.

"Excuse me!" he began, "but did you reach your destination safely?"

"My destination!" exclaimed Estelle. "What do you mean? I don't know you!"

"Perhaps not by name. But are you not the young lady whom I met some years ago in Portland, Oregon, inquiring how to get to New York?"

"You are mistaken," said Estelle, and her voice was frigid in tone. "I have never been in Portland in my life," and she turned aside.

CHAPTER XI

WONDERINGS

For a moment Lieutenant Varley seemed to hesitate, and Alice felt sorry for him. He was distinctly not of the type that would try to make an acquaintance in this way just because Estelle was a pretty girl. He seemed embarrassed and ill at ease. But he was not the sort of young man to give up, once he thought he was right, as he obviously did in this case. To do so, Alice felt sure he reasoned, would have been to acknowledge that he was just the sort he seemingly was not.

"I really beg your pardon," he went on, in a firm but respectful tone. "I am sure I have met you before. I do not wonder that you do not remember me, but I cannot forget you. Yours isn't a face one easily forgets," and he smiled genially, and in a manner to disarm criticism.

"But I never was in Portland," insisted Estelle, and it was plain that she was puzzled by his persistence but not offended by it. "And I don't remember ever having seen you before."

"Perhaps if I recall some of the circumstances to you it may bring back the memory," suggested the lieutenant. "Believe me, I do not do it out of mere idle curiosity, but you seemed in such distress at the time, and so uncertain of where you wanted to go, that I really wished after I had directed you that I had placed you in charge of the conductor of your train."

"But I never was in Portland," said Estelle again, "and though I have been in New York, I went there from Boston. Surely you have confused me with some one else."

The young officer shook his head.

"I couldn't do that," he said with a smile that showed his white, even teeth. "It was just about this time three—no, four years ago. I was in Portland on business, and as I entered the railroad station you were standing there—"

Estelle shook her head, smiling.

"Well, for the sake of argument," admitted the lieutenant, "say it was some one who looked like you."

"All right," agreed Miss Brown, and she and Alice drew near the porch railing, on the other side of which stood the officer with doffed hat.

"A young lady was standing there, and she seemed quite bewildered," went on Lieutenant Varley. "I saw that she was in some confusion, and asked if I could be of any service to her. She said she wanted to get to New York, but did not know which train to take. I asked her if she had her ticket, and she replied in the negative. I asked her if she wanted to buy one, and she said she did, showing a purse well filled with bills—"

"Then surely it could not have been I!" exclaimed Estelle with a merry laugh. "I never had a purse well-filled with bills. We moving picture players—at least in my class—don't go about like millionaires. Gracious! I only wish I did have a well-filled purse, don't you, Alice?"

"Surely. But what else happened? I'm interested in the story."

"And I was interested in the young lady," went on the officer. "I bought her ticket for her with the money she handed me, and put her on the train. She was quite young— about as old as you"—and he smiled at Estelle, "and I asked her if some one was going to meet her. She said she thought so, but was not sure, at any rate she felt that she could look after herself. I left her, and meant to speak to the conductor about her, but did not have time.

"I have often wondered since whether she arrived safely, and when I saw you sitting here I felt that I could ascertain. For I certainly took you for that young lady."

"I am sorry to spoil your romance," said Estelle, "but I am not the one. I never was farther West than Chicago, and then only for a little while, filling a short engagement in the movies."

"Well, I won't insist on your identity," said the lieutenant, "but I'm sure I'm not mistaken. However, I won't trouble you further—"

"Oh, it has been no trouble," interrupted Estelle. "I'm sure I hope you will find that young lady some day."

"I hope so, too," and the lieutenant bowed. But, judging from his face, Alice thought, it was plain that he was sure he had already found the young lady in question.

At that moment Mr. Pertell came out on the porch and saw

the lieutenant.

"Ah, I'm glad you are here," observed the manager. "I want to ask you a great many things. This staging of sham battles is not as easy as I thought it would be."

"We can have the sham battles all right," answered the officer, with a smile. "But I can imagine it is not easy to get good moving pictures of them. We have to operate over a large area, and we can't always tell what the next move will be. Though, of course, for the purpose of making views we can ignore military regulations and strain a point or two."

"That's just what I want to talk about," remarked Mr. Pertell. "In the attack, for instance, the way the plans have been made the sun is wrong for getting good views. Can't we switch the two armies around?"

"Well, I suppose we can. I'll speak to the colonel about it," and then the two went inside, where Mr. Pertell had his office in the parlor of the farmhouse.

"What do you think of him, Estelle?" asked Alice.

"Why, I think he's very nice, but he's altogether wrong about me."

"And yet he seemed so positive."

"Yes, that is what makes it strange. But I never saw him before—that is, as far as I know; and I'm certain I was never in Portland. He must be mistaken, but it was nice of him to admit it. I thought at first he was using the old method to get acquainted."

"So did I. But he isn't that kind."

Laura Lee Hope

"He doesn't seem to be."

Russ Dalwood came around the corner of the porch with Paul Ardite and Hal Watson, a young man lately engaged to play juvenile roles. Hal had become very friendly with the little group that circled around Ruth and Alice.

"You girls have an hour yet before you go on," Russ informed them. "We haven't anything to do until then, either. Want to take a run in to town? I've got to call at the express office for some extra film, and the auto is ready. Where's Ruth?"

"Up in her room. I'll go for her," offered Alice. "Shall we have time?"

"Plenty. You can even buy yourself some candy—or let us do it for you," laughed Paul.

"We'll let you do it!" said Estelle, as Alice hastened to summon her sister.

"Ruth! Ruth! where are you?" called Alice, as she ran upstairs—Alice seldom walked.

"Here, just reading over my new part. What's the matter?"

"We're going for an auto ride with the boys. Come along. You can study in the car."

"Yes, a lot of studying I could do under those circumstances. But I'll come—I want a bit of diversion. Who else is going?"

Alice told her, and then spoke about the young lieutenant.

"Wasn't it queer he should be mistaken?" she asked.

Ruth did not reply for a moment.

"Wasn't it?" repeated her sister.

"I was just wondering," said Ruth, slowly. "Was it?"

Laura Lee Hope

CHAPTER XII

AN INTERRUPTION

While Alice was putting on her hat Ruth looked at her in some surprise.

"Was it?" she repeated.

"Was what?" asked her sister.

"Was it a mistake?"

"Of course it was, Ruth! Didn't I tell you Estelle said he must have taken her for some one else, as she had never been in Portland in her life? Of course, it was a mistake. What makes you think it wasn't?"

"Because, Alice, I am beginning to have doubts regarding Estelle."

"Doubts! You don't mean about the ring?"

"Of course not! But I am beginning to think she is not altogether what she seems to be."

"What do you mean?"

"Well, nothing serious, of course. And if she has done what I think she has it isn't any worse than many girls have done, and have gained by it, rather than lost, though it was risky."

"You mean?"

"I mean that I believe she isn't telling us all she knows. She is hiding something about her past. And I believe it is that she has run away from home because her family would not let her go into moving pictures. You know we sort of suspected that before. Now, in that case, she would have every reason to deny that she had seen that young lieutenant in Portland."

"Why should she, providing I grant that you are right?"

"Because he might know her friends and would tell them where she was. And she doesn't want that known until she has made a reputation. I don't blame her. If ever I ran away—"

"Ruth! *you* are not thinking of it, are you?"

"Silly! Of course not. But if I should I wouldn't want to run back home until I had something to show for my efforts. It may be that way in Estelle's case. She doesn't want to return like the prodigal son."

"I believe you're entirely wrong," declared Alice. "What I think is that she perhaps comes of good people. When I say that I don't mean that they were any better than we are, but that they so regarded themselves, and would look askance at motion picture players. Well, Estelle doesn't want to bring any annoyance on her family, and that may be the reason she doesn't tell much about herself. But as for that young officer's having seen her, I believe Estelle when she says he

Laura Lee Hope

is mistaken. Don't you?"

"I don't know what to believe," returned Ruth. "But I'm not going to worry over it."

"And you won't tell her you don't believe she is what she seems to be?"

"Of course not, you little goose! But I'm going to keep my eyes open. You know we may be able to give her some good advice. You and I, Alice, don't meet with near the temptations that assail other girls in this business, and it's because father is with us all the while. Now Estelle isn't so fortunate; so I propose that we sort of look after her."

"Oh, I'm very willing to do that."

"And if we see anything that is likely to cause her trouble, we must shield her from it. That is what I mean by sort of keeping watch over her. At the same time, I believe that she is not altogether what she seems. She is hiding something from us—even though we are trying to be so kind to her. But she doesn't really mean to do it. She is just afraid, I think."

"And you really believe that lieutenant knows her?"

"He may. At least I think, from what you said, that he is honest in his belief. But we will watch and wait. We must try to help Estelle in the hour of trial."

"Of course we will. Now hurry, for they are waiting for us."

"Such a funny thing just happened to me!" cried Estelle to the party of young folks when they were in the automobile and on the way to the village. "I was mistaken for some one else."

"What—again?" asked Alice.

"No, the same incident that you witnessed," and she related the episode of the lieutenant as Alice had detailed it to Ruth.

"That was queer," commented Hal Watson.

"I should say so!" exclaimed Russ.

"Was he at all fresh?" Paul asked, and his air was truculent.

"Not in the least!" Estelle hastened to assure him. "He was honestly mistaken about it, that was all," and she enlarged on the incident, and seemed so genuinely amused by it that Alice nudged her sister as much as to say:

"See how much in error you are."

But Ruth only smiled, and Alice noticed that she regarded Estelle more closely than ever.

The party made merry in the town, going into the "Emporium," for ice-cream sodas; and even the presence of Maurice Whitlow at the other end of the counter, where he was imbibing something through a straw, could not daunt Alice's high spirits. Whitlow smiled and smirked in the direction of his acquaintances, but he received no invitation to join them.

As Estelle was going out in the rear of the party, the extra player slid up to her and asked:

"Mayn't I have the pleasure of buying you some more cream?"

"You may not!" exclaimed Estelle, not turning her head, and

there were snickers from the other patrons in the place. Maurice turned the shade of his scarlet tie, and slid out a side door.

"You're getting too popular," chided Alice to her friend. "First it's the young lieutenant, and now it's your former admirer."

"I can dispense with the admiration of both!"

"Even the lieutenant?" asked Ruth, meaningly.

"Oh, he wasn't so bad," and Estelle either was really indifferent, or she assumed indifference in a most finished manner that would have done credit to a more experienced actress than she was.

"What's the matter—are we late?" asked Paul, as, on the way back to Oak Farm, he saw Russ look at his watch and then speed up the car a bit.

"Yes, a little. Mr. Pertell said he wanted to begin that skirmish scene at eleven exactly, and it's ten minutes to that now. We can just about make it. The sun will be in just the right position for making the film. It's in a thicket you know, and the light isn't any too good. That's the scene you girls are in," he went on.

"Speed along," urged Paul. "I've got to get into my uniform and make up a bit."

There is very little "make up" done for moving pictures taken in the open, and not as much done for studio work as there is on the regular stage. The camera is sharper than any eye, and make-up shows very plainly on the screen. Of course, eyes are often darkened and lips rouged a bit to make them appear to better advantage. Even the men make up a little but not much. For close-up views, though, where the faces are more than life size, artistic make-up is very essential. The camera, in this case, is a magnifying glass, and the most peach-blow complexion would look coarse unless slightly powdered.

"We'll be all right if we don't get a puncture," said Hal.

No sooner were these words out of his mouth than there came a hiss of escaping air.

"There she goes!" cried Paul. "Stop, Russ!"

"No, we haven't time. I'm going to keep on. It's better to get in on the rims and cut a shoe to ribbons than to spoil the film."

They sped along in spite of the flat tire. And it was well they did, for Mr. Pertell was anxiously waiting for his players when they arrived at Oak Farm.

"You cut it pretty fine," was his only comment. "Don't do it again. Now get ready for that skirmish scene."

This was one little incident in the big war play. In it Ruth and Alice were to be shown driving along a country road. There was to be an alarm, and a body of Confederate cavalry was to encounter one of the outposts of the Union army. There was to be a skirmish and a fight, and the Union men were to be driven off, leaving some dead and wounded. The girls, though shocked, were to look after the wounded.

All was in readiness. The soldiers, some drawn from the newly-arrived National Guards, were posted in their respective places. Lieutenant Varley was to play the part of one of the wounded Unionists.

"All ready—come on with the carriage!" called Mr. Pertell to Ruth and Alice, who were waiting out of range of the camera. They had rehearsed the direction they were to take. "Go on!" called the director to Russ. "Camera!"

The grinding of the film began, and Ruth and Alice acted their parts as they drove along in the old-fashioned equipage. Suddenly, in front of them the bushes crackled.

"There they come!" cried Ruth, pulling back the horses as called for in the play. "The soldiers!"

But instead of a band of men in blue breaking out on the road, there came a herd of cows, that rushed at the carriage, while the horses reared up and began to back.

"Stop the camera! Stop that! Cut that out!" frantically cried Mr. Pertell through his megaphone. "Hold back those men!" he added to his assistant who had signaled for the Confederates to rush up.

CHAPTER XIII

FORGETFULNESS

Ruth and Alice for the moment were not quite certain whether or not this was a part of the scene. Very often the director would spring some unexpected effect for the sake of causing a natural surprise that would register in the camera better than any simulated one.

But these were real cows, and they did not seem to have rehearsed their parts very well, for they rushed here and there and surrounded the carriage, to the no small terror of the horses, which Ruth had all she could do to hold in.

"Oh, what shall we do?" cried Alice. "I'm going to jump out!"

"You'll do nothing of the sort!" exclaimed her sister. "Sit where you are! Do you want to be trampled on or pierced with those sharp horns, Alice?"

"I certainly do not!"

"Then sit still! This must be a mistake."

It did not take much effort on Ruth's part to make Alice

remain in the carriage with all those cows about. For she had learned on Rocky Ranch that while a crowd of steers will pay no attention to a person on a horse, once let the same person dismount, and he may be trampled down.

These, of course, were not wild steers—Alice could see that. But she thought the same rule, in a measure, might hold good.

More cows crashed through the bushes until the road was fairly blocked, and then came another rush of many feet and the Union skirmish party came galloping along. They had received no orders to hold back, and so dashed up.

At the same moment a ragged boy with a long whip came rushing up. Evidently, he was in charge of the cows, but when he saw the soldiers in their uniforms, a look of fear spread over his face.

"I didn't do nothin', Mister Captain! Honest I didn't!" he yelled. "These is pap's cows, an' I'm drivin' 'em over to the man he sold 'em to. I didn't do nothin'."

"Nobody said you did!" laughed Lieutenant Varley with a bow to Ruth and Alice in the carriage. "But why did you drive them in here to spoil the picture?"

"I didn't know nothin' about no picture—honest I didn't! I took this road because it was shorter. Don't shoot pap's cow-critters. I'll take 'em away."

"Well, that's all we want you to do," said Mr. Pertell, coming up with a grim smile. "You nearly got yourself and your cow-critters in trouble, my boy. Drive 'em back now, and we'll go on with the film. Did any of 'em get in, Russ?" he asked.

"Just a few, on the last inch or so of the reel. I can cut that out and go on from there. Hold the carriage where it is, Ruth," he called.

"All right," she answered, for she had now quieted the restive horses.

"Don't be afraid, boy," said Alice to the lad. "You won't be hurt."

"And won't they hurt pap's cow-critters, neither?"

"No, indeed. It was all a mistake."

"I—I didn't know there was no war goin' on," remarked the lad, as he sent an intelligent dog he had with him after the straying animals. "Me an' pap we lives away over yonder on t'other side of the mountain. An' we don't never hear no news. I was plum skeered when I seen all them ossifers. Thought sure I was ketched, same as I've heard my grandpap tell about bein' ketched in the army. He was a soldier with Sherman, and I've heard him tell about capturin' cow-critters when they was on the march."

"Well, this would be like old times to him, I suppose," said Mr. Pertell. "But this is only in fun, my boy—to make motion pictures. So take your cows away and we'll go on with the work. Drive 'em on," and the boy did so with a curious, backward look at the girls in the carriage, and at the Union soldiers, who were going back to their places to get ready anew for the skirmish charge.

"And this time we'll have it without cows," said Mr. Pertell. "They might go all right in a film of Sherman's march, but not in this skirmish fight. All ready now. Take your places again."

The preliminary advance of the carriage, containing Ruth and Alice had been filmed all right. Very little need be cut out. Once the cows were beyond the camera range, Russ again began grinding away at the film.

"Now come on—Union soldiers!" cried the director.

From their waiting place Lieutenant Varley led his men; and as they swept on past the carriage, Alice and Ruth registering fear, the Confederates rushed out to meet them.

Then began the skirmish. Guns popped. Horses reared, some throwing their riders unexpectedly, but this made it all the more realistic. Men fought hand to hand with swords, using only the flats, of course. Horses collided one with another, and the animals seemed to enter into the spirit of the conflict fully as much as did the men. There was a rattle of rifles, but no cannon were used in this scene.

Russ and his helpers filmed it, and, standing behind them watching the mimic fight, was the director, shouting orders through his megaphone and, when he could not make himself heard in this way, using a field telephone, calling his instructions to helpers stationed out of sight in the bushes, where they could relay the commands to those taking part in the skirmish.

"A little livelier now!" yelled Mr. Pertell. "Give way, you Union fellows, as though you were beaten, and then drive them back to the fight, Mr. Varley. That's the way!"

The conflict raged and the cameras clicked away. It was all one to the camera men—a parlor drama or a sanguinary conflict. So long as the shutter worked perfectly, as long as the focus was correct and the film ran freely, the camera men were satisfied.

"Now you Confederates pretend to be overwhelmed, and then rally with a rush and sweep the Unionists out of the thicket!" ordered the director.

This was done, and, all the while, at one side of the picture crouched Ruth and Alice, as two Southern girls. They had leaped from their carriage and were waiting the outcome of the conflict, stooping down out of the way of flying bullets.

This was a side scene in the war play, and did not involve the main story. Ruth and Alice, as did the other main characters, assumed various roles at times.

"Come on now! You Unionists are beaten. Retreat!" called the director, and Lieutenant Varley's men rode off, leaving him and some others injured on the field of the conflict.

It was here that Alice and Ruth took an active part again. Ruth rushed up to the fallen lieutenant and felt his pulse. No sooner had she done so than the director cried:

"Stop the camera! That won't do, Miss DeVere!"

"Why not?" she asked.

"Because you felt his pulse with your thumb. No nurse would do that. The pulse in the thumb itself is too strong to allow any one to feel the pulse in another's wrist. Use the tips of your first and second fingers. Now try again. Ready, Russ!"

This time Ruth did it right. It was characteristic of Mr. Pertell to notice a little detail like that.

"Not one person in a hundred would object to the pulse being felt with the thumb," he explained afterward; "but the hundredth person in the audience would be a doctor, and he'd know right away that the director was at fault. It is the little things that count."

Ruth and Alice busied themselves ministering to the wounded who were made prisoners by the Confederates. The lieutenant was put in their carriage and driven away. That ended the scene at the place of the skirmish.

"Very well done!" Mr. Pertell told the girls, as they prepared for the next act, which was in a room of a Southern house, whither the wounded had been carried.

These were busy days at Oak Farm. With the arrival of the two regiments of the National Guard, pictures were taken every day, leading up to the big battle scene, which had been postponed. When they were not posing for the cameras, the guardsmen were drilling in accordance with the regulations of the annual state encampment under the direction of the regular army officers.

"Well, have you quite recovered from your wounds?" asked Alice of Lieutenant Varley one day, as she met him outside the farmhouse.

"Oh, yes, thanks to the care of your sister and yourself. By the way, I hope your friend Miss Brown is not angry with me."

"Why should she be?"

"Well, because I thought I had seen her before."

"I don't believe she is. I haven't heard her say. But here she comes now. You can ask her," and Estelle came around the turn of the path. Seeing Alice talking with the lieutenant, she hesitated, but Alice called:

"Come on—we were just speaking about you."

"I wondered why my ears burned," laughed Estelle.

"Perhaps you two are going somewhere," said the officer, preparing to take his leave.

"Oh, to no place where you are not welcome," answered Alice, graciously, with a side look at her companion to see if Estelle objected. But the latter gave no sign, one way or the other.

"Thank you!" exclaimed the guardsman. "I have to take part in a little scene in about an hour, but I would enjoy a walk in the meanwhile. You are both made up, I see?"

"Yes, we are Southern belles to-day," laughed Alice.

"Belles every day," returned the lieutenant with a bow.

"Nicely said!" laughed Estelle. "You are improving!"

She and Alice wore the costumes of generations ago, big bonnets and hoopskirts.

"Let's go over and see what they're filming there," suggested Alice, pointing to where a crossroads store had been put up.

The scene at the store was one to represent a dispute among some Southerners and some Northern sympathizers. It was to end in a fight in which one man was to draw his revolver.

All went well up to the quarrel, and then it became too realistic, for, by some chance, there was a bullet in the

Laura Lee Hope

revolver instead of a blank cartridge, and it entered the leg of one of the disputants. He fell and bled profusely.

"Get Dr. Wherry!" yelled Mr. Pertell.

"Dr. Wherry went into the village this morning to get some stuff," Russ said, "and he hasn't come back yet."

"Then somebody will have to go after him!" cried the director.

"I'll go!" offered Alice. "I can take this horse and carriage!" for a rig was hitched outside the "store."

"I'll go with you!" cried Estelle, and then, in costume and made up for the pictures as they were, they got into the vehicle and drove off.

CHAPTER XIV

IN THE SMOKE

"Do you think he'll die?" asked Estelle, as she took the reins and flicked the horse lightly with the whip.

"I hope not," answered Alice.

"Did it make you faint to see the blood?"

"A little. Did it you?"

"Yes. I can't bear it! It makes me—Oh, it makes me—"

Estelle closed her eyes, and Alice was surprised to see her turn pale, even under her rouge, and shudder.

"That's queer," Alice said. "I should have thought, being on a ranch as you were, you might have become used to accidents and scenes of violence."

"Who said I was on a ranch?"

"Why, you did!"

"I did?"

Laura Lee Hope

"Yes; don't you remember? That day when we were talking about branding cows—"

"Oh, maybe I did. I'd forgotten. Oh, dear! here comes an auto, and I'm not sure about this horse. I'm afraid he'll start to rear."

At this intimation that there might be trouble, Alice's face took on a worried look, and she fore-bore to press the questions she had been asking Estelle.

The horse showed some signs of fear as he passed the automobile in the road, but the man driving the car was considerate enough to stop his machine and motion to the girls to pass. They did so, the horse getting as far to one side of the road as he could, his nostrils distended and his ears pricked forward.

"There! Thank goodness that's over!" sighed Estelle. "Now to make speed and get that doctor. I hope the man doesn't die."

"I do too," acquiesced Alice. "Did you see how sharply the man looked at us?"

"Who, the man that was shot?"

"No, the one in the auto. He stared and stared!"

"Probably he wondered where in the world we got a horse in these days that was afraid of an auto. I wonder myself where this steed has been in hiding. There are so many cars now that it is a wonder horses aren't using gasoline as perfume."

"No, he wasn't looking at the horse," persisted Alice. "He was looking at us. Perhaps he knew you, Estelle."

"Why do you say that? I'm sure I never saw him before. Maybe it was you he was staring at."

"No, it was you he was staring at, but I don't blame him. You are very striking looking to-day."

"It's this dress. Isn't it quaint?"

"And pretty! Oh, but we mustn't talk so frivolously when that poor man may be dying. We must drive faster."

"Talking isn't going to make the horse go any slower. In fact, I think maybe he'll go quicker to get the trip over with sooner so he can be rid of our chatter. But I don't think the poor man is badly hurt. He may bleed a lot, but they can hold that in check until we get the doctor."

They drove on, and were presently in the village. They had been told where Dr. Wherry had gone—to a drugstore to get some medical supplies—and thither they made their way.

"Do you notice how every one is staring at us?" asked Alice, as they drove along the streets.

"They do seem to be," admitted Estelle, looking for the drugstore. "I guess it's the horse; he is so bony he has many fine points about him, as Russ said. And we're queer looking in these costumes ourselves."

When they alighted at the pharmacy and started in, they became aware of the growing sensation they were creating. For a little throng had gathered in front of the store, and more men and boys came running up, to form in two lines— a living lane—through which Alice and Estelle had to pass.

"We certainly are creating a sensation," gasped Alice,

Laura Lee Hope

growing embarrassed.

"Look! a regular bridal crowd," said Estelle in a low voice.

Though they undeniably presented a pretty picture in their paint, powder, curls and hoopskirts, they were also an unusual one for that little country village.

"Look at the society swells!" cried one boy.

"Dat's de new fashion—makin' your nose look like a flour barrel!" added another.

"Aren't those dresses sweet?" sighed a girl.

"They must be the latest New York style," added a companion. "I heard that full skirts were coming in again."

"Well, ours are certainly full enough," murmured Alice, looking down at her swaying hoops.

And then some one guessed the truth.

"They're actresses—the movie actresses!" came the cry, and this attracted more attention than ever, for if there is one person about whom the American public is curious, it is the actor.

"Oh my!" exclaimed Estelle, "now we are in for it. Hurry inside the store!"

The girls fairly ran into the friendly shelter, and some of the crowd attempted to follow, but the drug clerks barred the way, guessing what the excitement was about.

"Dr. Wherry!" gasped Alice. "Is he here?"

"Right back there—in the prescription department," a clerk said. "Which of you is ill?"

"Neither one!" cried Estelle. "We want him for a man out at Oak Farm. He's been shot—an accident in the play. Tell him to hurry, please, and then show us some way of getting out through a side door. I can't face that crowd—this way," and she looked down at her elaborate hoop-skirted costume, which might have been all right in the days of sixty-three, but which was unique at the present time.

"What's the trouble?" asked Dr. Wherry, coming from behind the ground-glass partition. "Oh, Miss DeVere and Miss Brown!" he went on as he recognized the moving picture girls. "Is some one hurt?"

They told him quickly what the trouble was, and he cried:

"I'll go at once. You'd better come back with me in the auto if you don't want to run the gauntlet of the staring crowd. I'll bring my machine around to the side door."

"What about the horse we drove over?" asked Alice.

"I'll have Mr. Pertell send a man for that."

The girls, in their curiosity-exciting costumes, managed to slip out the side door and into the doctor's automobile without attracting the attention of the crowd. Then they made the trip back in good time and comfort.

"And to think we never for a moment thought of changing our things!" cried Alice, when they were at Oak Farm again.

"Or even of rubbing off some of the make-up," added Estelle. "But we were so excited—at least I was—when I saw the poor fellow hurt. I hope it is not serious."

"No, he's lost a little blood, that's all," said Dr. Wherry. "But I thought you were used to such scenes, Miss Brown, coming from the West, as you did."

"I from the West? Oh, yes, I have been there. Come on, Alice, let's see if they still want us for anything, and, if they don't, we'll change our clothes," and Estelle seemed glad of a chance to hurry away.

"I wonder," said Alice to her sister afterward, "whether she is really so squeamish as she pretends, or if she doesn't want it known that she is from the West?"

"It's hard to say. Estelle is acting more and more queerly every day, I think."

"So do I. Though I am quite in love with her. She has such a sweet disposition."

"Yes, she is a lovely girl. I only wish there wasn't that bit of mystery about her."

"And it is a mystery," went on Alice. "Every once in a while I catch Lieutenant Varley looking at her, when he thinks he isn't observed, and he shakes his head as though he could not understand it at all."

"Then you think he still feels sure she is the girl he met in Portland?"

"I'm positive he does, and he isn't doing it to further his own ends and force an acquaintance with her, either. He honestly believes he has met her before."

"Well, it is very strange. But she doesn't seem to want to talk about anything connected with her past."

"No, and I suppose we should not try to force matters."

The man who was shot was soon out of danger, and, meanwhile, the taking of the war scenes went on with some one else in his place. A number of sham engagements had been fought, all working up to the big final battle, in which Ruth would play her part as an army nurse, and Alice would act as the spy. Estelle, too, had been given a rather important part, much to the annoyance of Miss Dixon, who had been expecting it.

The vaudeville actress made sneering and cutting remarks about "extra players butting in," and there were veiled insinuations concerning the missing ring, but Estelle took no notice, and Alice, Ruth and her other friends stood loyally by her.

"We'll film that burning barn scene to-day," said Mr. Pertell one morning at the breakfast table, when he had ascertained that the atmospheric conditions were right. "That's the one where you two DeVere girls are surprised on your little farm by the visit of some Union soldiers. You have been caring for a wounded cousin, who has escaped through the Union lines, and at the news that the Yankees are coming you hide him in the barn. Then the Unionists set fire to it, and you girls have to drag him out.

"There'll be no danger, of course, for the fire won't be near you—in fact, the barn won't burn at all—only a shack nailed to it. And the smoke will be from the regular bomb. You have plenty of them, haven't you, Pop Snooks?"

"Oh yes, plenty of smoke bombs, Mr. Pertell."

All was soon in readiness for the burning-barn scene. Ruth and Alice received the wounded cousin (an inside scene this) and then, when an old colored mammie (Mrs. Maguire) came panting with the news that the Yankees were coming, the wounded Confederate was carried out to the barn. Then came the visit of the Yankees, who, suspecting the presence of the escaped prisoner, made diligent search, but without success.

"Fire the barn, anyhow!" cried the captain.

Then came the spirited scene where Ruth and Alice got their wounded relative out. He was a slim young man, and they could easily carry him, for he was supposed to be overcome by the smoke.

"Ready, Alice?" asked Ruth, as they went through the action called for in the script.

"Yes, ready. You take his head and I'll take his heels. Don't be too stiff," Alice admonished the young man. "We can carry you better if you're limp."

"I'll be limp enough if I swallow any more of that smoke," choked the actor. "It's fierce!"

Indeed, Pop Snooks had been very liberal in the matter of smoke bombs. Great clouds of the black vapor swirled here and there, and Ruth and Alice had to get free breaths whenever they could.

"Come on!" yelled the director through his megaphone. "Lively!"

Alice and Ruth, half carrying, half dragging, the wounded soldier, staggered out, Russ clicking away at the camera.

"Good! That's good! It's fine!" exclaimed the enthusiastic director.

Ruth was conscious that she was suddenly dragging more of the weight of the man's body than at first. But she thought one of Alice's hands had possibly slipped off, and she did not want to call a halt to get a better hold.

"My! But this is choking!" gasped Ruth.

Finally, she staggered out into the open, dragging the soldier by his shoulders. She slumped down on the ground, in a place free from smoke, and registered exhaustion.

"Where's Alice?" cried Paul, who was holding back in readiness for his appearance in the scene. "Where's Alice?"

"Isn't she there?" gasped Ruth, rising on her elbow.

"No, she isn't. She must be—"

"Hold that pose, Ruth! Don't stir or you'll spoil the scene!" yelled the director. "We'll get your sister!"

CHAPTER XV

THE HOSPITAL TENT

"The show must go on!" This is the motto of circus and theatrical performers the world over. No matter what happens, under what strain or pain the player labors, no matter what occurs short of death itself, the public must not be allowed to guess that anything is wrong. And sometimes even death itself has been no barrier—for players have gone through with their parts on the stage when, but the act previous, they have learned that some loved one had passed away.

And more than one clown has bounded into the sawdust ring with merry quip and jest, with a smile on his painted face, while his heart was breaking with grief.

And so it was with Ruth DeVere. As she staggered out of the smoke clouds and saw that Alice had not followed, at once the dreadful thought came to her that her sister had been overcome by the fumes. And, although the smoke bombs were harmless as regards fire, the breathing of the chemical fumes for any length of time might mean death.

Thus, as Ruth was about to stagger to her feet to go back into the murky cloud to look for Alice, there came the director's orders to "hold that pose!"

The show must go on! That meant it would not do to spoil the scene, ruin the film, and necessitate a retake if, by any possibility, it could be avoided.

"Stay where you are, Ruth! Stop the camera, Russ! Hold the pose—both of you. We'll go on from there when we get Alice out!"

And Ruth, her heart torn with anguish, must remain. She was glad her father was not present.

"Get in there and get the girl!" cried Pop Snooks who was busy lighting more smoke bombs. "Get that girl, some of you fellows!" For he had guessed in an instant what had happened. It was not the first time one of the players had been overcome by the heavy fumes.

Into the cloud dashed some of the head property man's helpers. Russ and Paul, who could leave their posts while the camera was not in motion, also penetrated the murkiness.

Fortunately, Alice had been overcome when within a few feet of the clear atmosphere, and it was the work of but an instant for Paul to carry her outside, where she could breathe pure air.

"The poor dear!" cried Mrs. Maguire. "Here, give her this ammonia and water."

"Don't come too close to her, Mrs. Maguire!" warned the director. "Your black make-up will come off on her face, and it will show in the film."

The director had to think of all those things, though it might seem a bit heartless.

"I'll be careful," promised the motherly old woman. "I'll be careful."

Alice sipped the aromatic spirits of ammonia, and felt better.

"Did I faint?" she asked. "How silly of me!"

"Are you all right?" asked Ruth, still in her place by the side of the soldier, who was supposed to be unconscious.

"Yes, Ruth dear. I'm all right now. Oh, and did I leave you to carry him all alone? I'm so sorry!"

"It was all right. I dragged him."

"Yes, the scene is all right," said Mr. Pertell. "Now, Alice, I don't want to be heartless, but will you be ready to go on in this, or shall we abandon it and make a retake?"

"Oh, I'll go on. Just a moment, and I'll be all right."

After a minute or two the plucky girl recovered from the effects of the smoke, and, though she was weak and wan, managed to go through her part. She and Ruth carried their "cousin" out of the burning barn which was then allowed to fall to ruins. Or rather, the extra part, built on for the purpose, was, Pop Snook's smoke bombs effectually concealing from the audience the fact that the real barn was not in the least harmed.

"Well, I'm glad that's over," said Alice with a sigh, as a little later she washed off her make-up and donned her ordinary clothes.

"Do you feel bad?" her sister asked.

"Yes, sort of choked."

"Then let's take a walk up on the hill where there is always a breeze."

On the grassy eminence with the fresh breezes blowing about them, Alice soon felt much better. But Mr. Pertell called off some of the scenes set down for next day, so that she might have a rest.

"We'll soon be ready for the big hospital scene, Ruth, and also for the one where you try to get away with the papers, Alice," said Mr. Pertell to the two girls one day. "And, in order that everything may run smoothly I've made a little change in the scenario. I'm going to have a preliminary hospital scene. In that you will be a sort of orderly, or assistant nurse, Ruth. And there comes an emergency in which you do so well that you are sent for to be a nurse in one of the big hospitals maintained near the front. That will make the story more logical.

"So we'll have one of those hospital scenes to-day. I'll stage a small engagement, and have a number of men wounded. They'll be brought in, and there will be a night scene. The doctors and other nurses go off duty, and you are in charge. An emergency occurs—maybe a bandage slips from an artery and you sit and hold the wound until a doctor can come and tie the artery again. We'll work it out as we go along."

"Is there anything for me?" asked Alice.

"No, your part will stand all right as it is until you get to the big hospital scene. Come on now, Ruth; we'll have a rehearsal."

The rehearsal went off well, and the little change promised to strengthen the story of the war play. The hospital was set up near Mr. Apgar's corn-crib.

"And maybe that'll be a good thing," he said. "If you folks use enough of them there disinfectants and carbolic acid, you may scare away all the rats and mice that eat my corn in the winter."

"Oh! will there be rats and mice?" asked Ruth, apprehensively.

"Not in the hospital," said Mr. Pertell with a laugh. "It will be strictly sanitary—as much so as things were in the days of sixty-three."

The fight between the two forces was staged some distance away from the hospital, and the guns soon began to rattle and to roar again. The girls did not mind them by this time, however.

This skirmish had no particular part in the general story, but it was filmed just the same, as it could be spliced in with the other fighting scenes.

"And you can't get too much of that," Mr. Pertell said.

Russ, with some helpers, was taking the fighting pictures preliminary to the hospital act. He was nearing the end of the reel in his machine when, to his dismay, he found he had forgotten to bring a spare one.

"Here, you!" he called to one of the extra soldiers lying lazily on the grass near the camera, "hop over and ask Pop Snooks to give you an extra reel for me."

The man did not answer.

"Don't you hear me?" yelled Russ, grinding away at the film which was being quickly used up. "Go and get me that reel!"

Still no response.

"Are you deaf?" shouted Russ, and then he thought perhaps the discharge of so many cannon had made the man unable to hear.

"Go over and punch that fellow!" cried Russ to Paul. "Wake him up, and tell him to get me that extra reel."

"All right," Paul assented. "I'd go myself only I have to carry a message to headquarters in a minute or two."

He ran over and kicked the soldier, who seemed to be asleep.

"Hi! What's the idea?" demanded the rudely awakened one.

"The camera man wants you to go to get him some film."

"Who—me?"

"Yes—you! Skip!"

"I can't go get no film!"

"You can't? Why not?"

"'Cause I'm dead, that's why! I was told to be killed, and I was. I fell off my hoss dead, an' I'm deader'n a door nail. I dassn't git up to git no film for nobody. I'm dead!"

And the man rolled over and closed his eyes.

CHAPTER XVI

A RETAKE

"What's the matter over there?" called Russ to Paul. "Is he going to get my film?"

"He says he can't."

"Can't? Why not? Has he lost his legs?"

"No. But he's dead. This is carrying realism to the extreme."

"Oh, good-night!" cried Russ. "I haven't but a few feet left. Make him go."

"I won't go I tell you," the man cried. "I was told to play dead, and I'm goin' to," and he stuck to the instructions he had received.

Fortunately, one of Russ' helpers was free a moment later, and he went for the extra roll of film, while the dead man enjoyed his part to his satisfaction.

"Well, he did just right," said Mr. Pertell, when told of the incident afterward. "I wish more performers would do exactly as they are told. Of course, I don't mean to say a player must slavishly do just as I tell him. But in some cases a dead man's coming to life might spoil a big scene."

Matters were now in readiness for the preliminary hospital scene. A ward had been fitted up in a shed where electric lights could be used to get the necessary illumination, the current being brought from town. In the shed were ranged white beds, in which a number of wounded men were reposing. Other men were in wheeled chairs, while still others sat up as if recovering from a long and dangerous siege from wounds. All were picturesquely bandaged.

The preliminary scenes had been taken. The doctor had made his rounds of the wounded on the cots. He had taken their temperature and had felt their pulses, while the other women of the company, as nurses, accompanied the surgeon on his journey. Other wounded were brought in.

Night settled down in the hospital. The big, hissing electric lights were turned off, and from outside a window "moonlight" streamed in. The moonlight, of course was made by another electric light, properly shaded.

"Now, I think we're ready for you, Ruth," said the director. "You are on duty alone in the ward when the emergency occurs."

In the glow of the beams of light from the window Ruth, on duty alone, took her place.

"All ready now!" called Mr. Pertell, from where he was standing behind Russ, who was grinding away at the camera. "You start from your half-doze, Ruth, and listen. Then you approach one of the cots and discover that the bandage has slipped and that the man is bleeding to death. You press on the artery, and finally rouse another of the hospital patients—one not badly wounded—and send him for the surgeon."

Ruth carried out the instructions perfectly. Her acting was so very natural that afterward, when the film was shown, more than one person found himself holding his breath lest Ruth should remove her thumb from the severed artery.

The slightly wounded man limped out to get the surgeon, who came rushing in, and the artery was tied. Then followed words of praise for Ruth. This laid the foundation for her summons to a larger hospital when the proper time came.

The next day more battle views were the order of the day. In one of these Estelle had to do some fast riding, to leap her horse across a ditch and speed away from pursuing troopers.

"Aren't you nervous for fear you'll fall?" asked Ruth, as the young horsewoman was making ready.

"Well, no. I don't think about that part. All I am afraid of is that I may get out of range of the camera. You see I'm not very old at this business."

"Just how did you come to get into it?" asked Alice.

"Why, it was a sort of accident. I was on a boat one day, leaning over the rail looking at the water, when a gentleman came up, begged my pardon for speaking without being introduced, and asked me if I had ever been in the movies.

"I hadn't, though I had often thought I would like to be, and I told him so. He asked me to call at his studio, and I did. They gave me a 'try out,' found I photographed well, and they cast me for small parts. Then they found out I could ride and they let me do some outdoor stuff. From then on I did very well, and when I heard your company was going to make a big war play, I applied to Mr. Pertell. He took me, I'm glad to say."

"And we're glad you're here," ejaculated Alice.

"We'll go out and watch you jump; it fascinates me, though it makes me afraid," Ruth declared. "My sister and I did some riding while we were at Rocky Ranch, but it was nothing to what you do."

"Oh, it takes practice, that's all," answered Estelle.

There were some animated scenes previous to the one in which Estelle took part. There was a fight over the possession of a bridge, and the Confederates, having driven off their enemies, prepared to blow it up to prevent the Union army from using it.

Estelle was to try to reach the bridge before it was destroyed, but, failing in that, she was to ride her horse to a narrow part of the stream and leap over.

All went well, and the time came for her to take her swift ride to try to reach the bridge. On and on she galloped, until she was met by a colored man who warned her of the fact that in another moment the bridge would be destroyed.

"She's going pretty close!" murmured Mr. Pertell, as he stood near Russ, who was filming the scene. "Some of those timbers may fall pretty near her."

But Estelle seemed to know no fear. She rode straight for the bridge, and she was only a short distance away when it blew up, the planks and rails flying high into the air.

Laura Lee Hope

Then she turned her horse to reach, ahead of her pursuers, the place she was to jump the stream. So near was she to the bridge that she had to swerve her horse quickly to avoid being struck by a fragment of the falling wood.

"Plucky girl, that!" murmured Mr. DeVere.

While Estelle was being filmed down by the stream, one of the assistant camera men, a new hand, prepared to take a scene where a Southern farmer rides up to warn the Confederate cavalry of Estelle's escape, so they may take after her. Maurice Whitlow was the farmer.

"Here, you!" cried Mr. Pertell to Whitlow, "ride down there and deliver the message—that's your part in this scene."

There was a small automobile which Mr. Pertell had been using standing near, and Maurice leaped into this and started across the field toward a detachment of the Southern cavalry.

Away rattled Maurice in the car, and the camera man ground away, showing the farmer on his way to give the warning. Suddenly Mr. Pertell turned and saw what was going on.

"For the love of gasoline, stop!" he cried. "The whole scene is spoiled. There'll have to be a retake! Of all the stupid pieces of work this is the worst! Stop that camera!"

CHAPTER XVII

ESTELLE'S STORY

"What's the matter?" cried Russ Dalwood, running back from the stream where he had been to see that an assistant was successfully getting the scene after Estelle had leaped to the other bank.

"Matter! Look!" cried the director, and he pointed to Maurice, speeding to carry his message in the small runabout.

"Good-night!" gasped Russ, who understood at once.

"Why, what's wrong with it?" asked Paul. "Isn't he running the machine all right?"

"Oh, he's running it all right," said Mr. Pertell in tones of disgust. "And that's just the trouble! I told him to jump on a horse with that dispatch, and he goes in the auto!"

"I suppose he thought it was quicker," commented Paul.

"Quicker! Yes, I should say it was! But I'll get him out of there quicker than he can shake a stick at a dead mule. The idea of riding in an auto to carry a message in Civil War days. Why, there wasn't a real auto in the whole world then.

How would it look in a film to see an up-to-date runabout butting in on a scene of sixty-three. Get him back here and make him start over again on a horse as he ought to," went on the director. "An auto in sixty-three! Next he'll be sending wireless telephone messages about fifty years before they were ever dreamed of!"

Fortunately, not much of the film had been reeled off, and the scene was one that could easily be made over. Estelle's leap was not spoiled, nor was the blowing up of the bridge.

"Huh! I didn't think anything about there not being autos in those days," said Maurice, when he had been brought back and mounted on a horse.

"That's just it," commented Mr. Pertell. "You've got to think in these days of moving pictures. The audiences are more critical than you would suppose. Even the children now laugh at fake scenes and incongruities. And as for using a dummy in danger scenes, it's getting harder and harder every day to get by with it. You stick to horses or to Shank's mules, young man, when it comes to transportation in this war film. No autos where they are going to show in the film."

That was only one of the many details the director and his assistants had to look after. If eternal vigilance is the price of liberty, it is much more so the price of good films. The camera sees everything in a pitiless light. It exaggerates faults and it refuses to shut its eye to anything at which it is pointed. The absolute truth is told every time.

Of course, there are trick films, but even then the camera tells the truth fearlessly. It is only the on-lookers' eyes that are deceived. The camera can not be fooled. And though a man may be seen to be shaking hands with himself or cutting off his own head, it is done by double exposure, and could not be accomplished were it not for the fact that the camera and the film are so fearlessly honest and truth-telling.

"What's the matter, Estelle?" asked Alice of the rider that afternoon, when they were in Ruth's room resting after the work of the day. "You seem to be in pain."

"I am. I strained my side a little in that water jump. Petro slipped a bit on the muddy bank."

"Did you do much jumping out West?" asked Ruth, while Alice was getting a bottle of liniment.

"In the West? I don't know that I ever jumped there. I can't remember—"

Estelle paused, and passed her hand across her eyes as though to shut out some vision.

"Are you faint?" asked Ruth.

"No—no, it isn't that. It—it is just that I—that I—Oh, I wonder if I can tell you?" and Estelle seemed in such distress that the two sisters hastened to her.

"What is it? Tell me, are you badly hurt?" asked Ruth. For she had known of performers who concealed injuries that they might not be laid off, and so lose a day's work. "What is the matter, Estelle?"

"It is my—my head."

"Did you fall? I didn't hear them say anything about it!" exclaimed Alice.

"No, it isn't that," and the girl looked from one sister to the

Laura Lee Hope

other. "Oh, I wonder if I dare tell you?"

"If there is anything in which we can help you, tell us, by all means!" answered Ruth, warmly—sympathetically. "But we don't want to force ourselves—"

"Oh, no! It isn't that. I'm only wondering what you will think of me afterward."

"We shall love you just the same!" cried impulsive Alice.

"Don't be too sure. But I feel that I must tell some one. I have borne all I can alone. It is getting to the point where I fear I shall scream my secret to the cameras—or some one!"

Then Estelle had a secret!

"Do tell us. Perhaps we can help you—or perhaps my father can," suggested Ruth.

"I don't believe any one can help me," said Estelle. "But at least it will be a relief to tell it. I—I am living under false pretenses!" she blurted out desperately.

"False pretenses!" repeated Alice. At once her mind flashed back to Miss Dixon's ring. Was it the taking of this that Estelle was hinting at? The girl must have guessed what was in the mind of her hearers, for she hastened to add:

"Oh, it isn't anything disgraceful. It's just a misfortune. You remember you have been asking me where I learned to ride—whether I didn't use to live on a ranch—questions like that. Well, you must have noticed that I didn't answer."

"Yes, we did notice, and we spoke about it," said truthful Ruth.

"We thought you didn't wish to tell," added Alice.

"Wish to tell! Oh, my dears, I would have been only too glad to tell if I could."

"Why can't you?" asked Ruth. "Are you bound by some vow of secrecy? Is it dangerous for you to reveal the past?"

"No, it is simply impossible!"

"Impossible!" the two sisters exclaimed.

"Yes, I can no more tell you what life I lived, where I lived, who I was, or what I was doing, up to a time of about three or four years ago, than I can fly."

"Why not?" asked Alice, puzzled.

"Because the past—up to the time I named—is a perfect blank to me. My mind refuses absolutely to tell me who I was or where I lived—who my people were—anything of the past. My mind is like a blank sheet of paper. I can remember nothing. Oh, isn't it awful!" and she burst into tears.

CHAPTER XVIII

"WHAT CAN WE DO?"

"You poor dear!" cried Alice, and she knelt down on the floor beside Estelle and put her arms about the weeping girl. Ruth, too, with an expression of sympathy, stroked the bowed head.

"We want so much to help you," Ruth murmured.

"Let me get you something," begged Alice. "Some smelling salts—some ammonia—shall I call any one—the doctor—?"

"No, I—I'll be all right presently," said Estelle in a broken voice. "Just let me alone a little while—I mean stay with me—talk to me—tell me something. I want to get control of my nerves."

Ruth did not seem to know what to say, but Alice pulled a small bottle from her pocket, and held it under Estelle's nose.

"It's the loveliest new scent," she said. "I bought a sample in town."

Estelle burst into a laugh, rather a hysterical laugh, it is true, but a laugh nevertheless. It showed that the strain and tension were relaxing to some extent.

"Isn't it sweet?" Alice asked.

"It is, dear. Let me smell it again. It makes me feel better," and Estelle breathed in deep of the odorous scent.

"How silly I was to give way like that," she went on. "But I simply couldn't help it. This has been going on for so long, and it got so I couldn't stand it another minute. How would you like it not to know who you are?"

"Not very much, I'm afraid," said Ruth, softly.

"That, in a way, is why it has been such a relief to be in the moving pictures," Estelle went on. "I could be so many different characters, and, at times, I thought perhaps, by chance, I might be cast for the very part I have lost—cast for my real self, as it were."

"You must have had a hard time," said Alice.

"I haven't told you half the story yet," Estelle went on. "Would you like to hear the rest?"

"Indeed we would!" exclaimed Ruth. "Not from any idle curiosity, but because we want to help you."

"And I do need some one to help me," murmured Estelle. "I am all alone in the world."

"You must have relatives somewhere!" insisted Alice.

"None that I ever heard of. But then, who knows what might have happened in the life that is a blank to me—in the life that lies beyond that impenetrable wall of the past?

"But I mustn't get hysterical again. Just let me think for a moment, so I may tell you my story clearly. I shall be all right in a moment or two."

"Let me make you a cup of tea," proposed Ruth. "I'll make some for all of us," and presently the little kettle was steaming over the spirit lamp, and the girls were sipping the fragrant beverage.

"Thank you. That was good!" murmured Estelle. "I feel better now. I'll tell the rest of my miserable story to you."

"Don't make it too miserable," and Alice tried to make her laugh a gay one.

"I won't—not any more so than I can help. I think it will do me good to let you share the mystery with me."

"Then it is a mystery?" asked Ruth.

"Somewhat, yes. You may think it strange, but I can not think back more than three years—four at the most. I am not at all certain of the time. But go back as far as I can, all I remember is that I was on a large steamer."

"On the ocean?" asked Alice.

"No, on the Great Lakes. I was going to Cleveland, which I learned when I asked one of the officers."

"And didn't you know where you were going before you asked?" Ruth questioned.

"I hadn't the least idea, my dear. I might just as well have been going to Europe. In fact, when I first looked out and saw the water, I thought I was on the ocean."

"But where did you come from, what were you doing there, where were your people?" cried Ruth.

"That's it, my dear. Where were they? I didn't know. No one knew. All I could grasp was the fact that I was there on the boat."

"Alone?"

"Yes, all alone."

"But who bought your ticket—who engaged your state-room?" questioned Ruth.

"That is the queer part of it. I did it myself. When I first became conscious that I was in a strange place I was so shocked that I wanted to scream—to cry out—to ask all sorts of questions. Then I realized if I did that I might be taken for an insane person and be locked up. So I just shut myself in my stateroom and did some thinking.

"The first thing I wanted to know was how I got on the steamer, but how to find that out without asking questions that the steamship people would think peculiar, was a puzzle to me. Finally, I decided to pretend to want to change my room, and when I went to the purser I asked him if that was the only room to be had.

"'Why no, Miss,' he said, 'but when you came on board and I told you what rooms I had, you insisted on taking that one.' That was enough for me. I realized then that I had come on board alone, and of my own volition, though I had not any recollection of having done so, and I knew no more of where I came from than you do now."

"How very strange!" murmured Alice. "And what did

you do?"

"Well, I pretended that I had been tired and had not made a wise choice of a room, and asked the purser to give me another.

"'I thought, when you picked it out, you wouldn't like that one,' he said to me, 'but you looked like a young lady who was used to having her own way, so I did not interfere.'"

"That was another bit of information. Evidently, I looked prosperous, a fact that was borne out when I examined my purse. I had a considerable sum in it, and the large valise I found in my room was filled with expensive clothes and fittings. Yet where I had obtained it or my money or my clothes I could not tell for the life of me. All I knew was that I was there on board the ship."

"And did you change your stateroom?" asked Ruth.

"Yes; the purser gave me another one. And then I sat down and tried to puzzle it out. Why was I going to Cleveland? I knew no one there, and yet I had bought a ticket to that port—or some one had bought it for me."

"Did that occur to you?" asked Alice. "That some one might have had an object in getting you out of the way."

"Well, if they had, they took a very public and expensive method of doing it," Estelle said. "I was on one of the best boats on Lake Erie, and I had plenty of money."

"Did you find in what name your room was taken?" asked Ruth. "That might have given you a clue."

"The name given was Estelle Brown," was the answer. "I

gave that name myself, for I recognized my handwriting on the envelope in which I sealed some of my jewelry before handing it to the purser to put in his safe. Estelle Brown was the name I gave."

"And was it yours?" asked Alice.

"I haven't any reason to believe that it was not. In fact, as I looked back then, and as I look back now, the name Estelle Brown seems to be my very own—it is associated closely with me. So I'm sure I'm Estelle Brown—that is the only part I am sure about."

"But what did you do?" asked Ruth. "Didn't you make some inquiries?"

"I did; as soon as I reached Cleveland. At first I hoped that my memory would come back to me when I reached that place. I thought I might recognize some of the buildings. In fact, I hoped it would prove to be my home, from which I had, perhaps, wandered in a fit of illness.

"But it was of no help to me. I might just as well have been in San Francisco or New York for all that the place was familiar to me. So I gave that up. Then I began to look over the papers to see if any Estelle Brown was missing. But there was nothing to that effect in the news columns. All the while I was getting more and more worried.

"I went to a good hotel in Cleveland and stayed two or three days. Then I happened to think that perhaps my clothes might offer some clue. I examined them all carefully, and the only thing I found was the name of a Boston firm on a toilet set. At once it flashed on me that I belonged in Boston. I seemed to have a dim recollection of a big monument in the midst of a green park, of narrow, crooked streets and historical buildings.

"Then, in a flash it came to me—I did belong in Boston. How I had come from there I could not guess, but I was sure I lived there. So I bought a ticket for there and went as fast as the train could take me.

"But my hopes were dashed. Even the sight of Bunker Hill monument did not bring the elusive memory, nor did viewing the other places of historic interest. Yet, somewhere in the back of my brain, I was sure I had been in that city before. I went to the place where my toilet set was bought, but the man had sold out and the new owner could give me no information.

"I did not know what to do. My money was running low, and I had not a friend to whom to turn. I happened to go in to see some moving pictures, and the idea came to me that perhaps I could act. I had rather a good face, so some one had hinted."

"You do photograph beautifully," said Alice.

"That's what one of the managers in Boston told me when I applied to him," said Estelle. "He gave me a small part, and then I learned that New York was really the place to go to get in the movies, so I came on, with a letter to a manager from the Boston firm.

"It must have been my face that got me my first engagement, for now I know I couldn't act. But, somehow or other, I made good, and then I got this engagement with Mr. Pertell.

"And that is my story. You can see what a strange one it is— for me not to know who I am. I'm almost ashamed to admit it, and that is why I have been avoiding all references to my past. But now I have told you, what do you think?"

"I think it's just terrible!" cried Alice. "The idea! Not to know who you are."

"The question is," said Ruth, "what can we do to help you? This must not be allowed to go any further. Valuable time is being lost. We want to help you, Estelle. What can we do? We must try to find out who you are."

"Yes, but how can you?" asked the strange girl.

Laura Lee Hope

CHAPTER XIX

A BIG GUN

Ruth did not answer for several seconds. She seemed to be thinking deeply, and Alice, who was fairly bursting with numberless questions she wanted to ask, respected her sister's efforts to bring some logical queries to the fore.

"Then your hopes that Boston would prove to be your home were not borne out?" asked Ruth, after a bit.

"No, but even yet I feel sure that I have lived at least part of my life in Boston, or near there. One doesn't have even shadowy memories of big monuments and historic places without some basis; and it was not the memory of having seen pictures of them. It was a real vision."

"And the name Estelle Brown?"

"Oh, I'm sure that belongs to me. It seems a very part of myself."

"Did you tell any of this to Mr. Pertell or to the other moving picture managers?" asked Alice.

"No. You are the first persons to whom I have told my

secret," Estelle said. "I was afraid if I mentioned it they might make it public for advertising purposes, you know. They might make public the fact that a young actress was looking for herself and her parents. I never could bear that!"

"But you want to find your folks, don't you?" asked Alice.

"That's the queer part of it," Estelle replied. "I seem never to have had any relatives. The way I feel about it now, I would never know that I had had a father or a mother. I seem to have just 'growed,' the way poor Topsy did in Uncle Tom's Cabin. That is another strange part of my present existence. I seem to be in a world by myself, and, as far as I can tell, I have always been there."

"What about Lieutenant Varley?" inquired Alice.

"Lieutenant Varley?" and Estelle's voice showed that she was puzzled.

"The young officer who said he met you in Portland."

"Oh, yes. I had forgotten. Well, I have absolutely no recollection of that, and I'm sure I would remember if I had been in the West. I'm certain I never was there."

"And yet if you weren't in the West how did you learn to ride so well?" Ruth queried.

"That's another part of the puzzle, my dear. Riding seems to come as natural to me as breathing. I don't seem ever to have learned it any more than I learned how to dance. I seem always to have known how."

"There's only one way to account for that," Alice said.

"How?"

"From the fact that you must have started to learn to ride and to dance when you were very young—a mere child."

"I suppose that would account for it. And yet, I can't remember ever being a child. I don't recall having played with dolls or having made mud pies. For me my existence begins about three or four years back, and goes on from there, mostly in moving pictures."

"It is a queer case," commented Ruth. "I don't know what to do to help you. Perhaps it would be a good thing to speak to Mr. Pertell about it. Often when children have been kidnapped, you know, their pictures are flashed on the screen in hundreds of cities, and sometimes persons in the audiences recognize them. That might be done with you, Estelle."

"No, I wouldn't dream of doing that. Perhaps something may turn up some day that will tell me who I really am. And perhaps I shall be sorry for having learned."

"No, you will not!" declared Alice. "You come of good people—one can easily tell that."

"Thank you, dear. And now I have inflicted enough of my troubles on you. Let's talk about something pleasant."

"You haven't burdened us with your troubles, Estelle dear," insisted Ruth. "It is a strange story, and we are interested in the outcome."

"Indeed we are," said Alice. "We want very much to help you."

"That's good of you. But I don't see what you can do. I'm just a sort of Topsy, and Topsy I'll remain. Now please don't say anything about what I have told you to any one—not even to your father—unless I give you permission. I don't want to be the object of curiosity, as well as of suspicion."

"Suspicion!" cried Alice.

"Yes, about Miss Dixon's ring."

"Oh! no one in the world believes you took that—not even Miss Dixon herself. I believe she has found the old paste diamond, and is too mean to admit it!" cried impulsive Alice.

"You mustn't say such things!" objected her sister.

"Well, neither must she, then. Oh, Estelle! Wouldn't it be great if you should prove to be the daughter of a millionaire!"

"Too great, my dear. Don't let's think about it. But I feel better for having unburdened some of my troubles on you. And if you will still be as nice to me as you always have been—"

"Why shouldn't we be?" asked Ruth.

"Oh, I don't know, but I thought—"

"Silly!" cried Alice, as she threw her arms about the strange girl and kissed her.

Suddenly, from a distant hill, came a dull, booming sound, that, low as it was, seemed to make the very ground tremble.

"What's that?" cried Alice.

Laura Lee Hope

"Thunder," suggested Ruth.

"It sounded more like an explosion," asserted Estelle.

"There it goes again!" exclaimed Alice.

"Look!" cried her sister.

She pointed through the open window, and as the girls peered out they saw the top of the hill fly upward in a shower of dirt and stones.

Once more the deep boom sounded.

"It's a big gun!" cried Alice. "I remember, now. Mr. Pertell said he wanted pictures of a siege of a fort, and he sent for a big gun to get explosive effects. Come on over!"

"And be blown to pieces?" objected Ruth. "Don't dare go, Alice DeVere!"

"Oh, come on! There's no danger. Russ is going to make the films. I guess they're just trying it now. It's too late to make good pictures. Come on."

"I'll go," offered Estelle. "I don't mind the noise."

Ruth declined to go, so the other two girls set off. On the porch they met Russ and Paul, who confirmed their guess that it was a big siege gun which Mr. Pertell had sent to New York to get, so he might show the effect of explosive shells.

"I'm going to film some to-morrow," Russ said.

"Be careful," urged Alice. "Don't get blown up!"

"I'm no more anxious for that than any one," laughed Russ, and together they set off toward the place where the big gun was being tried out.

Laura Lee Hope

CHAPTER XX

A WRONG SHOT

The big gun which Mr. Pertell had secured to make more realistic the war play he was preparing for the films, was an old fashioned siege rifle, made toward the close of the Civil conflict. It had not been used more than a few times, and then it had been stored away in some arsenal. The director, hearing of it, had secured it to fire at a certain hill on Oak Farm.

This hill would, in the motion pictures, form a stronghold of the Southern forces and it would be demolished by shells from the large cannon, and then would follow a charge on the part of the Union soldiers.

Real shells, with large explosive charges in them, would be used, but it is needless to say that when the shots were fired at the hill the players taking the parts of the Southerners would be at a safe distance.

"They're just trying it out now," observed Russ, who with Paul, was walking over the fields with Alice and Estelle. "Mr. Pertell wants to get the range, and decide on the best places from which to make the pictures. I think we'll film some to-morrow if it's a good day."

"What's the matter with your eyes, Estelle?" asked Paul, as he looked at her. "Were you working in the studio to-day? I know those lights always affect my sight."

"Why, no, I wasn't in the studio," and then Estelle realized why her eyes were so inflamed—it was from crying. She gave Alice a meaning glance, as though to enjoin silence, but she need have had no fears. Alice would not betray the secret.

The big gun had been mounted on a level piece of land, not far from the hill, and on this plain had been thrown up earthworks behind which the Union forces would take their stand in an effort to reduce the Confederate stronghold.

"They're going to fire!" cried Estelle as they came within sight of the gun, and saw, by the activities of the men about it, that a shot was about to be delivered.

Alice covered her ears with her hands, and Russ and Paul stood on their tiptoes and opened their mouths wide.

"What in the world are they doing that for?" asked Estelle.

"I can't hear a word you say!" called Alice, making her voice loud, to overcome her own hearing handicap.

"There she goes!" cried Russ.

The earth trembled as flames and smoke belched from the muzzle of the cannon, and the girls screamed.

Something black was seen for an instant in the air amid the swirl of smoke, and then another portion of the hill was seen to lift itself up into the air and dirt and stones were scattered about.

"A good shot!" observed Russ, letting himself down off his tiptoes. "That would make a dandy scene for the film."

"That's right," agreed Paul, also letting himself down and closing his opened mouth.

"Why did you do that?" asked Estelle, when the echoes of the firing had died away. "Why did you stand on your toes, and open your mouths?"

"To lessen the shock to our ear drums," answered Paul. "It is the concussion, that is, the rushing back of air into the vacuum caused by the shot, that does the damage. By opening your mouth you equalize the air pressure on the inside and the outside of your ear drums, just as you do when you go through a river tunnel. When there is a partial vacuum outside your ear, the air inside you presses the drum outward, and by opening your mouth—or by swallowing you make the pressure equal. Sometimes the pressure outside is greater than the pressure inside, and you must also equalize that before you can be comfortable."

"But that wasn't why you stood on your toes," Alice said.

"No; we did that to have less surface of our bodies on the ground so the vibration would be less. If one could leap up off the earth at the exact moment a shot was fired it would be much better, but it is hard to jump at the right instant, and standing on one's toes is nearly as good. Then you present only a comparatively small point which the vibrations of the earth, caused by the explosion of the gun, can act upon."

"That's a good thing to remember," Estelle said. "Are they going to fire again?"

"It looks so," observed Russ. "But if they knock away too

much of the hill there won't be any left for the pictures to-morrow."

"I believe they want to make the top of the hill flat," said Paul. "They are going to have some sort of hand-to-hand fight on it after the Unionists capture it," he went on. "I heard Mr. Pertell speaking of it."

"There goes another!" cried Alice, as she saw the same preparations as before and one man standing near the gun to pull the lanyard, which, by means of a friction tube, exploded the charge.

Once more the projectile shot out and, burying itself in the soft dirt of the hill, threw it up in a shower.

"That'll save me a lot of work!" exclaimed a voice behind the young people, and, turning, they saw Sandy Apgar smiling at them. "That's a new way of plowing," he went on. "It sure does stir up the soil."

"Won't it spoil your hill?" asked Alice.

"Not so's you could notice it. That hill isn't wuth much as it stands. It's too steep to plow, and only a goat could find a foothold on it to graze. So if you moving picture folks level it for me I may be able to raise some crops on it. Shoot as much as you like. You can't hurt that hill!"

The men at the gun signaled that they were going to fire no more that day, and then, as it was safe, the young folks made a trip to see the extent of damage caused by the shells.

Great furrows were torn in the earth and the stones, and the top of the hill, that had been rounding, was now quite flat, though far from being smooth.

The next day had been set for filming the scenes with the big gun in them. Contrary to expectations, no pictures could be taken, as the throwing up of the earthworks had not been finished. But a number of men from both "armies" were set to work, and as it afforded good practice for the militia they were called on to dig trenches, throw up ridges of earth, and go through other needful military tactics.

The girls had no part in the scenes with the big gun, except that, later on, they were to act as nurses in the hospital tent.

On top of the hill a force of Confederates would be stationed, and they were to reply to the fire of the big gun. Of course, when the projectiles struck the hill the soldiers would be a safe distance away, but by means of trick photography scenes would be shown just as if they were sustaining a severe bombardment.

"Is everything ready?" asked Mr. Pertell, a few days after the setting up of the big gun, during which interval a sort of fort had been constructed on the hill and a redoubt thrown up.

"I think so," answered Russ. "We couldn't have a better day, as far as sunshine is concerned. I'm ready to film whenever you are."

"I'll give the word in a minute. Paul, you're in charge of a detachment of Union soldiers that storms the hill as soon as the big gun has silenced the battery there."

"Very well, sir."

The big gun rattled out its booming challenge and was replied to by volleys from the rifles of the Confederates on the hill and by their field artillery, which they hurriedly brought up.

Shot after shot was fired, and one after another the Confederate cannon were disabled. They were blown up by small charges of powder put under them, set off by fuses lighted by the Confederates themselves, but this did not show in the picture, and it looked as though the Southern battery was blown up by shots from the big gun.

"All ready now, Paul! Lead your men!" yelled the director, who was standing near Russ and his camera. "Rush right up the hill. Stop firing here!" he called to those in charge of the big gun.

But something went wrong, or some one misunderstood. As Paul was charging up the hill at the head of his little band, Russ, turning his head for an instant, saw a man about to pull the lanyard of the big gun.

"Don't shoot! Don't shoot!" he yelled. "It's aimed right at Paul and his fellows!"

But Russ was too late. The man pulled the cord. There was a deafening roar, a cloud of smoke, a sheet of fire, and a black projectile was sent hurtling on its way against the hill, up the side of which Paul was climbing with his soldiers.

Laura Lee Hope

CHAPTER XXI

THE BIG SCENE

Nothing could be done! No power on earth could stop that projectile now until it had spent itself, or until it had struck something and exploded.

Horror-stricken, those near the big gun looked across the intervening space. How many would survive what was to follow?

The man who had pulled the lanyard sank to the ground, covering his face with his hands.

For a brief instant Paul, leading his men, looked back at the sound of the unexpected shot. He had been told that no more were to be fired. Doubtless, this was an extra one to make the pictures more realistic. But when he saw, in a flash, something black and menacing leaping through the air toward him and his men, instinctively he cried:

"Duck, everybody! Duck!"

He fell forward on his face and those of his men who heard and understood did likewise.

Ruth, Alice and Estelle, who were watching the scene from a distant knoll, hardly understood what it was all about. They had thought no more shots would be fired when Paul began his charge, but one had boomed out, and surely that was a projectile winging its way toward the partly demolished hill.

"That is carrying realism a little too far," said Ruth. "I hope—"

"Paul has fallen!" cried Alice. "Oh—something has happened!"

One must realize that all this took place at the same time. The firing of the shot, the realization that it was a mistake, Paul's flash of the oncoming projectile, his command to his men and the vision had by the girls. All in an instant, for a shot from a big gun does not leave much margin of time between starting and arriving even when fired with only a small charge of powder for moving picture purposes.

And, so quickly had it happened that Russ had not stopped turning the crank of his camera, nor had an assistant on the hillside, where he had been stationed to film Paul and his soldiers.

And then the projectile struck. Into the soft dirt of the hillside it buried its head, and then, as the explosion came, up went a shower of earth and stones. And ever afterward the gunner who inserted that charge blessed himself and an ever-watchful Providence that he had put in but half a charge, the last of the powder.

For it was this half-charge that saved Paul and his men. The projectile struck in the hill a hundred feet below where Paul was leading his force up the slope, and though they were well-nigh buried beneath a rain of sand and gravel, they were not otherwise hurt—scratches and bruises being their portion.

"What are they trying to do, kill us?" cried a man, staggering to his feet, blood streaming from a cut on his cheek.

"This is too much like real war for me!" yelled another throwing down his gun. "I'm going to quit!"

"No you don't!" shouted Paul. "Come on. It was a mistake. They won't fire any more. It will make a great scene on the film. Come on!"

He gave one look back toward the Union battery and saw Mr. Pertell fluttering a white flag which meant safety. Waving his sword above his head, Paul yelled again:

"Come on! Come on! It's all right! Up the hill with you! That shot was only to put a little pep in you!"

"Pep! More like sand! I got a mouthful!" muttered a sergeant.

"Get every inch of that. It's the best scene we've had yet, though it was a close call!" telephoned Mr. Pertell to the operator on the side of the hill. "Film every inch of it!"

"All right! I'm getting it," answered the camera man and he went on grinding away at his crank.

The explosion of the shell had, for the moment, stopped the advance of Paul and his men up the hill, but this momentary halt only made it look more realistic—as though they really feared they were in danger, as indeed they had been. Now the director called:

"It's all right, Paul! Go ahead! Keep on just as if that was part of the show."

"It was a lively part all right!" and Paul laughed grimly. "Come on, boys!"

And the charge was resumed.

Back of the dismantled battery, whence they had presumably been driven by the fire from the big gun, the Confederates were massed. They were waiting for Paul's charge, and they, too, had been a little surprised by the unexpected firing of the shell.

But now, in response to a signal on the field telephone, they prepared to resist the assault.

"Come on, boys! Beat the Yankees back!" was the battle cry that would be flashed on the screen.

Then came the fierce struggle, and it was nearly as fierce as it was indicated in the pictures. Real blows were given, and more than one man went down harder than he had expected to. There were duels with clubbed rifles, and fencing combats with swords, though, of course, the participants took care not to cut one another.

In spite of this, several received minor hurts. But this result only added to the effectiveness of the scene, though it was painful. But in providing realism for motion pictures more than one conscientious player has been injured, and not a few have lost their lives. It is devotion of no small sort to their profession.

Back and forth surged the fight, sometimes Paul's men giving way, and again driving the Confederates back from the crest of the hill. Small detachments here and there fired volleys of blank cartridges from their rifles, but there was not as much of this for the close-up pictures as there had been for the larger battle scenes. For while smoke blowing over a big field on which hundreds of men and horses are massed makes a picture effective, if seen at too close range it hides the details of the fighting.

And Mr. Pertell wanted the details to come out in this close-up scene.

Back and forth surged the fight until it had run through a certain length of film. Then the orders came that the Confederates were to give up and retreat. Before this, however, a number of them had been killed, as had almost as many Union soldiers.

Then came a spirited scene. Paul, leading his men, leaped up on the earthworks of the Confederate battery, cut down the Southern flag—the stars and bars. In its place he hoisted the stars and stripes, and with a wild yell that made the fight seem almost real, he and his men occupied the heights.

"Well done!" cried Mr. Pertell, enthusiastically, when he came over from the ramparts of the big gun. "Are you sure none of you was hurt when that shell exploded?"

"None of us," answered Paul. "It fell short, luckily, and the dirt was soft. No big rocks were tossed up, fortunately, and we came out of it very nicely."

"Glad to hear it. I've discharged the man who fired the gun."

"That's too bad!"

"Well, I hired him over again—but to do something else less

dangerous. I can't afford to take chances with big cannon. But I think the scene went off very well. That stopping and the bursting of the shell made it look very real."

"That's good," Paul said, wiping some of the dirt and blood off his face, for he had been scratched by the point of some one's bayonet.

That ended this particular scene for the day, and the players could take a much-needed rest. Plenty of powder had been burned, and the air was rank and heavy with the fumes.

"Are you sure you're all right, Paul?" asked Alice, when he came up to the farmhouse later in the day.

"Well, I think I'd be better if you would feel my pulse," he said, winking at Russ. "And you don't need to be in a hurry to let go my hand. I sha'n't need it right away."

"Silly!" exclaimed Alice, as she turned, blushing, away.

"It must have been a shock to you," said Ruth.

"It was. But it was over so quickly I didn't have time to be shocked long. Now, let's talk about something nice. Come on in to the town, and I'll buy you all ice-cream."

"That will be nice!" laughed Estelle.

It was several days later that Mr. Pertell, coming to where the moving picture girls and their friends were seated on the porch, said:

"The big scene is for to-morrow. In the hospital. This is where you are looking after the wounded officer, Ruth, and Alice, on pretense of being a nurse seeking to give aid, comes in to get the papers. I want this very carefully done, as it is one of the climaxes of the whole play. So we'll have some rehearsals in the morning."

"Am I to do that riding act?" asked Estelle.

"Yes, you'll do the horse stunt as usual. There's to be a cavalry charge, Miss Brown, so don't get in their way and be run down."

"I'll try not to," she answered.

CHAPTER XXII

ALICE DOES WELL

Long rows of wounded men lay stretched out on white cots in the hospital. Some wore bandages over their heads all but concealing their eyes. Others were so entwined with white wrappings that it was hard to say whether they were men or oriental women. Still others raised themselves on their elbows, spasms of pain corrugating their brows, while red cross nurses held to their lips cooling drinks.

Here at the bedside of one stood a grave surgeon, slowly shaking his head as he came to the melancholy conclusion that a further operation was useless. Over there they were carrying out a motionless form on a stretcher, a sheet mercifully draped over what was left. At the entrance to the hospital other bearers were carrying in those who came from the scene of the distant firing.

The boom of big guns shook the frail shack that had been turned into a hospital. Now and then, as the wind blew in fitful gusts, there was borne on it the acrid smell of powder. And again, in some dark corner of that building of suffering, there could be seen through the cracks, left by hasty builders, the flash of fire that preceded the booming crash of the cannon.

Laura Lee Hope

A sad-faced woman in black moved slowly down the line of cots led by a sympathetic nurse. She came to one bed, stopped as though in doubt, passed her hand over her face as if she did not want to admit that what she saw she did see, and then she fell on her knees in a passion of weeping, while the surgeons turned away their heads. She had found what she had sought.

From the farther door there entered a man, limping on crutches improvised from the limbs of a tree. Stained bandages were about one arm and another leg. His head, too, was wrapped so that only half his face showed. A hurrying orderly met him.

"You can't come in here!" he cried.

"Why not, I'd like to know. Ain't this the horspital?"

"Of course it is."

"Then why can't I come in here. I'm hurt, and hurt bad, pardner. Shot through leg and arm, and part of my jaw gone. Why can't I come in?"

"'Cause you can't. Didn't we just carry you out for dead? What'll the audience think if they see you walking again? Git on out of here!"

"I will not! I've wrapped this bandage around my head on purpose so they won't know me. Let me come in, will you? That's real lemonade them pretty nurses is givin' out to drink, and I'm as dry as a fish. I've been firin' one of them guns until I've swallowed enough smoke to play an animated cannon ball. Let me in the horspital."

"Yes, let him in!" called Mr. Pertell through his megaphone.

He was at the far end of the shack that had been hastily erected on Oak Farm as a hospital, for the last big scenes of the war play, "A Girl in Blue and A Girl in Gray."

"All right, just as you say," answered the orderly. "Come on in, Bill. Are you going to die this time?"

"I am not! I'm going to be one of them converts, and get chicken sandwiches and jelly."

"You mean convalescent."

"Um. That's it! Lead me to me bed, will you, for I'm a sadly wounded old soldier—that's what I am."

Amid laughter he was led to a cot, where a smiling nurse tucked him in between the yellow sheets. For, as has been said, yellow takes the place of white in inside scenes.

And this was an inside scene, powerful electric lights dispelling all shadows so the cameras could film every motion and expression.

"Now remember!" called Mr. Pertell when the "wounded man," one of the extra players, had been comfortably put to bed, "remember no smiling or laughing when we begin to make the picture. This is supposed to be serious."

The rehearsal went on and finally the director announced that he was satisfied. Then the scenes were enacted over again, but with more tenseness and with a knowledge that every motion was being filmed with startling exactness.

"Now, Ruth, you come on!" called Mr. Pertell. "We've made a little change from the original scenario. You're to relieve Miss Dixon, who has been on this case. He's one of the

Northern officers, you remember, and he has with him papers that the Confederacy would do much to get.

"They are under the officer's pillow, you know. He is afraid to let them out of his possession. You must humor him, though you know that the papers will soon have to be taken away as he is to be operated on. It is here that Alice, as the spy, gets her chance. She pretends to be one of the nurses of this hospital, dons the uniform, and comes in here to get the papers. Are you ready?"

"Yes," answered Ruth.

Then the big hospital scene began.

Ruth, in her garb of a nurse, took her place at the side of the injured officer's cot. She felt his pulse, took his temperature and administered some medicine. Then the injured man, who was Mr. DeVere himself, sank back on his pillows. His hand went under the mass of feathers and brought out a packet of papers. At this point a close-up view was taken, showing on the screen the papers in magnified shape, so that the audience could note that they were Civil War documents. It was these that the officer was afraid would fall into the hands of the Confederates, so he kept them ever near him.

Ruth made as if to remove them when he had placed them under the pillow again, but he awoke with a start and prevented her. This was to show that it was necessary for some one to take them while the operation was being performed.

Then the scene changed to show Alice preparing for her work as a spy. The camera was taken to another part of the hospital, Ruth and her father having a respite, though they maintained their positions.

"Did I do all right, Daddy?" asked Ruth.

"Very well, indeed. You are getting to be a good actress. I wish you were on the speaking stage."

"I like this ever so much better. I never could speak before a whole crowd."

Alice was shown making her way into the hospital, a previous scene having depicted her as promising the Confederate officer in whose employ as a spy she was, that she would get the papers. She entered the hospital, pretending to be in search of a missing relative. Then, watching her chance, she prepared a sleeping powder for a tired and half-sleeping nurse off duty and prepared to take her uniform.

Alice played her part well. The sleeping nurse aroused, took the drugged drink, and went more soundly to sleep than ever. Then Alice was shown in the act of taking off the uniform. Another scene showed her walking boldly into the ward room to relieve Ruth.

There was a little scene between the two sisters, and Ruth registered that Alice must be very careful not to alarm or shock the wounded man who was soon to undergo the operation.

Alice acquiesced, and then sat down beside the cot. Slowly and carefully, like some pickpocket, she inserted her fingers under the pillow. Amid a tenseness that affected even the actors working with her, Alice took out the papers, inch by inch, and began to move away with them.

It was at this point that she was to be discovered by Paul, in the next bed. He had, in a previous scene, supposed to have taken place several months before, saved Alice's life, and they had fallen in love, Alice promising to wed him after the war. He supposed her to be a true Northern girl, and now he discovered that she was a Southern spy.

There was a strong scene here. Paul leaped from his bed, and tried to get the papers away from Alice. She, horror-stricken at being discovered as a spy by her lover, is torn between affection for him and duty to the South. She throws him from her, as he is weakened by illness, and is about to escape with the papers, when she fears Paul is dying and she is stricken with remorse. She decides to give up her task for the sake of her lover.

Slowly and softly, without awakening the old officer, she puts the papers back under his pillow and then, stooping over Paul, who has fainted from loss of blood, she kisses his forehead and goes out in a "fadeaway."

"Good! Great! Couldn't be better!" cried Mr. Pertell, as Alice came out of range of the camera. "That was better than I dared to hope. This will make a big hit!"

CHAPTER XXIII

A BAD FALL

"Have you made up your mind yet, Estelle?"

"No, Ruth! I haven't. I don't know what to do."

The two girls were in Estelle's room. Miss Brown was putting some protective padding under her outer garments, for in a little while she was to take part in a desperate ride— one of the last scenes in the big war play—a ride that had a part in a cavalry charge that was to be made by the desperate Confederates on the hosts of Unionists, who were closing in on their enemies. It was to be the last battle—a final stand of the Southern States, and they were to lose.

But Estelle was to make a desperate ride to try to save the day. This time she was to pose as a daughter of the South. The ride would necessarily be a reckless one, and Estelle felt that she might fall; so she was preparing for it.

"I don't know what to do," she went on to Ruth, who was helping her. "Sometimes I feel like doing as you and your sister suggest, and let your father into the secret—and Mr. Pertell too—and have them try what they can do to discover who I am.

"Then again, as I think it over, I'm afraid. Suppose I should turn out to be some one altogether horrid?"

"You couldn't, my dear, not if you tried. But if you don't want my father to know, and would rather work out this mystery yourself, why, I won't say another word."

"I want to think about it a little more," Estelle said.

They had been talking about her strange case, and the possible outcome of it. Alice had suggested that a motion picture story be written around it.

"It could be called 'Who is Estelle Brown?'" Alice said, "and it could be a serial. You could pose in it, Estelle, and make a lot of money. And, not only that, but you'd find out who your relatives were, I'm sure."

"Oh, I couldn't do it!" Estelle had cried. "I'd like the money, of course. I never was so happy as when I found I had a purse full when I was on that Cleveland boat! But I could not capitalize my misfortune that way."

"No, I was only joking," said Alice. And so the matter had gone on. Now Ruth had broached the subject again, and Estelle was still undecided.

"Wait until after this big ride of mine," she said. "Then I'll make up my mind. I really do want to know who I am, and I think, after this engagement, if I don't find out before, I'll go to Boston again. I'm sure my people are from that vicinity."

So it was left.

From outside came the stirring notes of a bugle. At the sound of it Ruth and Estelle started.

"That's the signal," said the latter. "I must hurry."

"I'll help you," offered Ruth, and she assisted in the tying of the last strings, and the snapping of the final fastenings of the suit of protective padding the rider wore.

"You don't take part in the actual charge, do you?" asked Alice, who came in at this point.

"Well, I have to ride ahead of the Union forces for a way," Estelle answered. "But I'm not afraid. Petro will carry me safely, as he has done before."

The girls went down and out into the yard. Off on the distant meadow of Oak Farm, which had been turned into a battlefield for the time being, were two hostile armies. The two regiments of cavalry were to meet in a final clash that was to end the war. There was to be the firing of many rifles and cannon. There were to be charges and countercharges. Men would fall from their horses shot dead. Certain horses, trained for the work, would stumble and fall, going down with those who rode them, the men having learned how to roll out of the way without getting a broken arm or leg. In spite of their training and practice, nearly all expected to be scratched and bruised. However, it was all part of the game and in the day's work.

"All ready now!" called Mr. Pertell. "We're going to have the first skirmish, and, after that, Miss Brown, you are to do your ride. Are you ready?"

"Yes," Estelle told the director.

The signal was given through the field telephone and then, with his ever-present megaphone, the director began to issue his orders.

The rifles cracked, the big guns rumbled and roared, smoke blew across the battlefield and horses snorted and pawed at the ground impatient to be off and in the charge. To them it was real, even though their masters knew it was only for the movies.

Bugles tooted their inspiring calls, and the officers, who knew the significance of the cadence of notes, issued their orders accordingly.

"Deploy to the left!" came the command to a squad of Union cavalry, and the men trotted off, to try a flank movement. Then came the firing of a Confederate battery in a desperate attempt to scatter the Union forces.

All the camera men in the employ of the Comet Film Company were engaged this day, and Russ was at his wits' end to keep each machine loaded with film, and to see that his own was working properly.

Pop Snooks had never before been called on to provide so many "props" as he was for this occasion, but he thoroughly enjoyed the work, and when, at the last minute, he had to make a rustic bridge whereon two lovers had a farewell before the soldier rode off to battle, the veteran property man improvised one out of bean poles and fence rails that made a most artistic picture.

"They'll have to get up the day before breakfast to beat Pop Snooks!" exclaimed Russ, admiringly.

All was now ready for the big cavalry charge.

"All ready!" came the order from Mr. Pertell. "Cameras!"

And the cranks began to work, reeling off the sensitive film.

The two bodies of cavalry rushed toward one another, hoofs thundering, carbines cracking, sabres flashing in the sun, white puffs of smoke showing where the cannon were firing.

"Now Miss Brown!" yelled the director, above the riot of noise. "This is where you make the ride of your life!"

"All right!" answered the brave girl, and, giving rein to her horse, she dashed off ahead of a detachment of cavalry that was to try to intercept her.

On and on rode Estelle. Ruth and Alice, who had finished their part in this scene, stood on a little hill, watching her.

On and on dashed Estelle, doing her part well, and foot after foot of the film registered her action. She was almost at the end now. She reached the Confederate ranks, gave over the message she had carried through such danger, and then, turning her horse, dashed away.

How it happened no one could tell. But suddenly Petro stumbled, and though Estelle tried to keep him on his feet she could not.

"Oh—oh!" gasped Ruth. "Look!" and then she turned her head away so as not to see.

Alice had a flash of Estelle flying over the head of her falling horse, and then, unable to stop, the rushing soldiers on their horses rode over the very place where Estelle had fallen.

CHAPTER XXIV

A DENIAL OF IDENTITY

Confused shouts, cries, and orders echoed over the field, Mr. Pertell, dropping his megaphone, rushed toward the scene of the accident, calling on Russ to follow and yelling back an order to have the stretcher men and the doctor follow him.

Dr. Wherry was even then waiting in readiness, for it had been feared that this big scene might result painfully, if not dangerously, for more than one. Some men had also been detailed as stretcher bearers and were in waiting.

"Shall we film this?" asked one of Russ's helpers, as the former dashed past on his way to help Estelle.

"No. Don't take that accident. It won't fit in with the rest of the film. It's all right up to that point, though. We can make a retake of the last few feet if we have to."

Even in this time of danger and suspense it was necessary to think of the play. That must go on, no matter what happened to the players.

"Go on with the cavalry charge—farther over!" directed Mr. Pertell, when he arrived on the scene and found a group of men about the fallen girl. "You can't do any good here. We'll look after her. I can't delay any longer on this scene. Go on with the charge, and carry out the program as it was outlined to you. Russ, you look after the camera men."

"What about Estelle?"

"Dr. Wherry and I will see to her."

The girl's golden hair was tumbled about her head, having come loose and fallen from under her hat in her fall. She lay in a senseless heap at one side of her horse. The animal had not gotten up, and at first it was thought he had been killed. But it developed that Estelle had trained him to play "dead" after a fall of this kind, and the intelligent creature must have thought this was one of those occasions.

"Easy with her, boys," cautioned the director, as the stretcher men tenderly picked up the limp form. "She may have some broken bones."

They placed her carefully on the stretcher and bore her to the hospital. Mrs. Maguire was ready to assist the trained nurse, who was kept ready for just such emergencies.

"The poor little dear!" exclaimed the motherly Irish woman. "Poor little dear!"

Meanwhile, the cavalry charge went on. Estelle had done her part in this. Was it the last part she was to play?

Ruth and Alice asked themselves this as they hurried toward the hospital.

"Oh, if she should be killed!" gasped Ruth.

"Wouldn't it be dreadful? And no one to tell who she really is," added Alice. "We must go to her."

"Yes, as soon as they will let us see her," agreed Ruth.

Dr. Wherry and the trained nurse were busy over the injured girl. A quick examination disclosed no broken bones, but it could not yet be told whether or not there were internal injuries. They could only wait for her to recover consciousness and hope for the best. All that could be done was done.

"Plucky little girl!" murmured Mr. Pertell, when told that Estelle was resting easily, but was still insensible. "She must have seen that she was going to have a bad fall, but she kept on and saved the film for us. We won't have to retake her scene at all—merely cut out the accident. Do your best for her, Dr. Wherry."

"I will, you may be sure."

Ruth and Alice were told that they could see Estelle as soon as she recovered consciousness, and it was safe for visitors to be admitted. And several hours after the accident the nurse, Miss Lyon, came to summon them from their room, where they were waiting.

"She has opened her eyes," Miss Lyon said.

"Did she ask for us?" Alice asked.

"I can't say that she did. She seems dazed yet. Sometimes in falls like this, where the head is injured, it is days before the patient realizes what has happened."

"Is her head injured?" Ruth inquired.

"Yes, she seems to have received a hard blow on it. Whether there is a fracture or a concussion Dr. Wherry had not yet determined. It will take a little time to decide. Meanwhile, you may see her, just for a moment."

Alice and Ruth softly entered the room where Estelle lay on a white bed. Her face was pale, but her eyes were bright. There was a subtle odor of disinfectants, of opiates and of other drugs in the room—a veritable hospital atmosphere.

"Don't startle her," cautioned the nurse, motioning for silence.

"We'll be careful," promised Alice, in a whisper.

The two sisters approached the bed. Estelle looked at them but, strange to say, there was no look of recognition in her eyes. Ruth and Alice might have been two strangers for all the notice Estelle took of them.

"She—she doesn't know us," whispered Ruth.

"She will, as soon as you speak," said Miss Lyon. "Just talk to her in a low voice, but naturally. She'll know you then, I'm sure."

"How—how are you feeling?" asked Ruth, in a whisper.

There was no response—no light of recognition in the eyes.

"A little louder and call her by name," suggested the nurse.

"You try, Alice," Ruth whispered.

Her sister stepped to the bedside.

"Estelle, don't you know me?" Alice asked.

The eyes turned in the direction of the voice.

"Were you speaking to me?" came the question, and both Ruth and Alice started at the changed tones of their friend.

"Yes, to you," Alice answered.

"I—I *don't* know you," was the gentle response.

"Don't you know me—Alice DeVere? And this is my sister, Ruth. Don't you know us, Estelle?"

"Is your name Estelle?" came the query.

"No, that is *your* name," and Alice smiled, though a cold hand seemed to be clutching at her heart. "That is your name —you are Estelle. Don't you remember?"

"Estelle what? Who is Estelle?"

"You are. You are Estelle Brown! Don't you know your own name?"

The golden head on the white pillow was slowly moved from side to side. The bright eyes showed no sign of recognition. Then came the gentle voice:

"I am not Estelle Brown. I don't know her. What do you mean? I don't know any of you. Why am I here? What has happened? I wish you would take me home at once. I live at the Palace."

"What—what does she mean?" gasped Ruth, looking in alarm at the nurse.

"I don't know. Perhaps she is delirious and imagines she is playing in the moving pictures. Was there a palace scene?"

"Not since she joined the company. But why does she deny her identity?"

"I can not say. Sometimes after an injury like this happens, people say queer things. We had better not disturb her further. I'll call Dr. Wherry."

Alice made one more effort to bring recollection to Estelle.

"Don't you know me, dear?" she asked softly. "I am Alice— your friend Alice. This is Ruth, and you are Estelle Brown, from Boston, you know."

"Boston? I was never in Boston. And I am not Estelle Brown. You must be mistaken."

Her eyes roved around the hospital room, and a look of pain and fright dimmed them. Then, seeming to fear that she had been unkind, she said gently to Alice:

"I am sorry I do not know you, for you are trying to help me, I am sure. But I never heard the name Estelle Brown. I am not she—that is certain. If you would only take me home! My people will be worried. We live at the Palace and—"

She tried to raise herself up in bed. A look of pain came over her face, and she fell back with closed eyes.

"She has fainted!" cried Miss Lyon. "I must get Dr. Wherry at once! Don't disturb her!"

She hastened off, while Ruth and Alice, not knowing what to think, went softly from the room.

CHAPTER XXV

REUNION

"Nothing but a passing fancy," said Dr. Wherry, later in the day, when Ruth and Alice questioned him about Estelle. "When a person has received a hard blow on the head, as Estelle has, the memory is often confused. She will be all right in a day or so. Rest and quiet are what she needs."

"Then she is in no immediate danger?" asked Mr. Pertell.

"None whatever, physically. She came out of that fall very well, indeed. The blow on her head stunned her, but the effects of that will pass away. She has no internal injuries that I can discover."

The last scenes of the war play were taken. The Confederates, after their final desperate stand were driven back, surrounded and captured. The "war" ended.

The regiments of cavalry took their departure. The extra players were paid off and left. A few simple scenes were yet to be taken about Oak Farm, but the big work was over, and every one was glad, for the task had been no easy one.

"Does Estelle yet admit her identity?" asked Ruth of Dr.

Wherry, two days after the accident.

The physician scratched his head in perplexity.

"No, I am sorry to say she doesn't," he answered. "She does not seem to recognize that name. I wish you and your sister would come in and speak to her again. It may be she will recognize you this time. A little shock may bring her to herself. I have seen it happen in cases like this."

Ruth and Alice again went to the hospital. Estelle was still in bed, but she seemed to be better. But, as before, there was no sign of recognition in the bright eyes that gazed at the two moving picture girls.

"Don't you know me—us?" asked Alice, gently.

"Yes. You were here before, soon after I was brought here," was the answer.

"Oh, Estelle! don't you know us!" cried Ruth, in horror.

"Whom are you calling Estelle?"

"Why, you. That is your name."

"I am not she. You must be mistaken! Oh, I wish they would take me home. I want father—mother—I want Auntie Amma. Oh, why don't they come to me?"

Ruth and Alice looked at one another. What did it mean? This babbling of strange names? Was it possible that they were on the track of discovering the identity of the girl who now denied the name she had given?

"Who is your father?" asked Ruth.

Laura Lee Hope

"And who is Auntie Amma?" inquired Alice.

"Why, don't you know? They live with me at the Palace. And my doll. Why don't you bring my doll?"

"She is delirious again," whispered the nurse. "You had better go. Evidently, she thinks she is a child again. Her doll!"

"I want my doll! Why don't you bring me my doll?" persisted the stricken girl.

"What doll do you want?" asked Alice.

"My own doll," was the reply. "My dear doll that I always have in bed with me when I am ill; my doll Estelle Brown!"

"Estelle Brown!" cried Ruth, in sudden excitement. "Is that the name of your doll?"

"Yes! Yes! Bring her to me, please!"

"Who gave you that doll?" asked Ruth, and she waited anxiously for the answer.

"My doll—my doll Estelle Brown. Why, my daddy gave her to me, of course. My father!"

"And what was your father's name?" asked Ruth in a tense voice.

She and Alice and the nurse leaned forward in eager expectation. They all recognized that a crisis was at hand. Would the stricken girl give an answer that would be a clue to her identity—the identity she had denied? Or would her words trail off into the meaningless babble of the afflicted?

"What is your father's name?" Ruth repeated.

The girl in the bed raised herself to a sitting position. She looked at the DeVere sisters—at the trained nurse. In her eyes now there was not so much brightness as there was weariness and pain.

And also there was more of the light of understanding. She looked from one to the other. Her lips moved, but no sound came from them. It was a tense moment. Would she be able to answer? Would the obviously injured brain be able to sift out the right reply from the mass of words that hitherto had been meaningless?

"What is your father's name?" repeated Ruth in calm, even tones. "Your father who gave you the doll, Estelle Brown? Who is he?"

Like a flash of lightning from the clear sky came the answer.

"Why, he is Daddy Passamore, of course!"

"Passamore!" gasped Alice. "Passamore?"

"Is your name Passamore?" whispered Ruth.

"Yes, I am Mildred Passamore. My father is Jared Passamore of San Francisco. I don't know why I am here, except that I was hurt in the railroad accident. If you will telegraph to my father, at the Palace Hotel, San Francisco, he will come and get me. And please tell him to bring my doll, Estelle Brown.

"I know it seems silly for a big girl like me to have a doll," went on the injured one. "But ever since I was a child I have had Estelle with me when I was ill. I am ill now, but I feel better than I did. So telegraph to Daddy Passamore to bring

Estelle Brown with him when he comes for me. And tell him I was not badly hurt in the wreck."

And with that, before the wondering eyes of the nurse, of Alice and of Ruth, Estelle Brown—no—Mildred Passamore, turned over and calmly went to sleep!

For an instant those in the hospital room neither moved nor spoke. Then Alice cried:

"That solves it! That ends the mystery! I'll go and get the paper."

"What paper?" asked Ruth.

"Don't you remember? The old paper that I wrapped my scout shoes in when we were packing to come to Oak Farm. The one that father saved because it had a theatrical notice of him in it.

"It was that four-year-old paper which contained an account of the strange disappearance of the wealthy San Francisco girl, Mildred Passamore. Don't you remember? There was a reward of ten thousand dollars offered for her discovery."

"Oh, I do remember!" gasped Ruth. "And this is she!"

"Must be!" declared Alice. "She says that's her name. And from what she told us she can, as Estelle Brown, think back only about four years. She must have received some injury that took away her memory. Now she is herself again.

"Ruth, I believe we have found the missing Mildred Passamore! We must tell daddy at once, and Mr. Pertell. Then we must telegraph Mr. Passamore. I'll get his address from the old paper. But the Palace Hotel, San Francisco, will reach him, I presume. Oh, isn't it all wonderful!"

"It certainly is," agreed Ruth.

They gave one glance at the sleeping girl—Mildred or Estelle—and then went out, while Miss Lyon summoned Dr. Wherry to acquaint him with the strange turn of the case.

"Mildred Passamore found! How wonderful!" exclaimed Mr. DeVere, when his daughters told him what had happened. "But we must make sure. It would be a sad affair if we sent word to the father, and it turned out that this girl was not his daughter. We must make sure."

Alice got out the old paper. It contained a description of the missing Mildred Passamore, and in another newspaper dated a few days before the one Alice had used as a wrapper for her shoes (another paper which Mr. DeVere had saved because of a notice in it) was a picture of the girl.

"It is she! Our girl—the one we knew as Estelle Brown—is Mildred Passamore!" cried Alice as she looked at the picture in the paper.

"There is no doubt of it," agreed Ruth, and Mr. DeVere affirmed his daughters' opinions.

Mr. Pertell was told of the occurrence, and, being a good judge of pictures and persons, he decided there was no doubt as to the identity.

"We will telegraph to Mr. Passamore at once," decided the director.

The crisis—for such it was in the case of the injured girl—seemed to mark a turn for the better. She slept nearly forty-eight hours, awakening only to take a little nourishment. Then she slept again. She did not again mention any names, nor, in fact, anything else. Her friends could only wait for the arrival of Mr. Passamore to have him make sure of the identity.

He had sent a message in answer to the one from Mr. Pertell saying that he and his wife were hastening across the continent in a special train.

"That means he hasn't found his daughter up to this time," said the manager, "and there is every chance that this girl is she."

Three days after her startling announcement Estelle or Mildred, as she was variously called, was much better. She sat up and seemed to be in her right mind.

"I don't in the least know what it is all about, nor how I came here," she said, smiling. "The last I remember is being in a railroad train on my way from San Francisco to visit relatives in Seattle. There was a crash, and the next I knew I found myself in bed here. I presume you brought me here from the train wreck."

"Yes, you were brought here after the—the—ah, accident," said Mr. Pertell, lamely.

"The nurse tells me you are a moving picture company," went on Mildred. "I shall be interested to see how you act. I always had a half-formed desire to be a moving picture actress, but I know Daddy Passamore would never consent to it."

"And she's been in the films for three years or more, and doesn't remember a thing about it!" murmured Alice. "Goodnight!"

"Alice!" rebuked her sister. But Alice, for once, did not care for Ruth's rebuke. Her astonishment was too great. And it was a queer case.

"We must be very careful!" said Dr. Wherry when, after a swift ride across the continent, Mr. Passamore and his wife reached Oak Farm. "We must not startle the patient."

"Oh, but I want to see my little girl!" cried the mother, with tears in her eyes. "My little girl whom I thought gone for ever!"

"I hope this will prove to be she," said Mr. DeVere.

"I'm sure it will!" cried the father. "No one but Mildred would remember her old doll—Estelle Brown!" and he held up a battered toy.

Softly, the parents entered the room. The girl on the bed heard some one come in, and sat up. There was a look of joy and happiness on her face; and yet it was not such as would come after a separation of four years. It was as if she had only separated from her loved ones a few hours before.

"Oh, Daddy! Momsey!" she cried. "I did so want you! And did you bring Estelle Brown?"

"My little girl! My own little lost girl!" cried Mrs. Passamore. "Oh, after all these years—when we had given you up for dead!"

"After all these years? Why, Momsey, I left you only two days ago to go to Seattle. There must have been a wreck or something; for I heard a dreadful crash, and then I awakened here with these nice moving picture folk. They were on the same train, I guess."

Laura Lee Hope

Dr. Wherry made the parents a signal not to tell the secret just yet.

"And did you bring Estelle?" asked Mildred.

"Yes, here is your doll!" and as Mr. Passamore handed it to his daughter he and his wife exchanged tearful glances of joy. The lost had been found.

It was a scene of rejoicing at Oak Farm, and the moving picture girls came in for a big share of praise. For had it not been for the fact that Alice had seen the paper containing the account of the missing girl and saved it, the identity of Mildred might not have been disclosed for some time.

Finally, she was told what had happened; that for four years she had been another person—Estelle Brown—a name she had taken after the awakening following the railroad accident because of some kink in the brain that retained the memory of the doll.

"Then Lieutenant Varley was right, he must have seen you in Portland," said Alice, when explanations were being made.

"He must have," admitted Mildred. "But I don't understand how it happened."

Later on it was all made clear.

Mildred Passamore, the daughter of a wealthy family, living temporarily at the Palace Hotel, in San Francisco, had started on a trip to visit relatives in Seattle. She was well supplied with money.

The train Mildred was on was wrecked near Portland, Oregon, and the girl received a blow on her head that caused her to lose her sense of identity completely. She did not seem to be hurt, and she was not in need of medical aid. Without assistance, she got on the relief train that took the injured in to Portland, and there it was that Lieutenant Varley saw her in the station.

Through some vagary of her brain, Mildred imagined she wanted to go to New York, and, as she had plenty of money, she bought a ticket for that city, the one to Seattle having been lost. Lieutenant Varley had helped her and, though he suspected something was wrong with the young lady the impression with him was not very strong until it was too late to be of assistance to her.

So, her identity completely lost, Mildred started on her trip across the continent. What happened on that journey she never could recollect clearly. That she got on the Great Lakes and then went to Boston was established. The reason for that was that, as a child, she had lived there. This accounted for the toilet set her mother had given her, and for the recollection of the monument and the historic places.

Why she was attracted to moving pictures could only be guessed at, but she "broke in," and "made good." Her ability to ride was easily explained. Her father owned a big stock farm, and Mildred had ridden since a child. But all this, as well as other remembrances of her younger days, was lost after the injury to her head in the railroad accident. She retained but one strongly marked memory—the name of her doll, the name which she took for her own.

So, as a new personage, she came to Oak Farm, unable to think back more than four years, and totally without suspicion that she was the missing Mildred Passamore. That she was not recognized as the missing girl was not strange, since the search in the East had not been prosecuted as vigorously as it had been in the West.

Mr. and Mrs. Passamore, hearing that the train on which their daughter was traveling had been wrecked, hastened to Portland, but there they could find no trace of Mildred. Lieutenant Varley, who might have given a clue, had sailed for Europe the day after his meeting with Mildred. Then began the search which lasted four years, and had now come to an end at Oak Farm.

"And to think that I have been two persons all this while!" exclaimed Mildred, when explanations had been made, and she was on the road to recovery. "But what made my memory come back?"

"The same thing that took it from you," explained Dr. Wherry. "It was the blow you received on the head when you fell from your horse. There had been a pressure on your brain, from the railroad crash, and the fall from your horse relieved it, so you came to yourself."

"Oh, I wonder if I could have taken Miss Dixon's ring in my second personality?" asked Mildred one day, when various happenings were being explained to her.

"No, you didn't!" exclaimed Alice. "It was found down under the carpet, back of her bureau. A maid discovered it there when cleaning. And that snip of a Miss Dixon left without apologizing to you."

"Oh, it doesn't matter, since I am not Estelle Brown, and my doll doesn't care what they say about her!" laughed Mildred. Miss Dixon and her friend had left Oak Farm to go back to New York, for their part in the pictures was finished for the time being.

"And to think that I really became a movie actress, after all!" laughed Estelle. "I think I shall continue in it, Daddy! It must be fun, though I don't recollect anything about it."

"No you sha'n't!" laughed Mr. Passamore. "Your mother and I want you at home for a while."

There is little more to tell.

Mildred Passamore rapidly recovered her health and strength. Her part in the pictures was finished and though he did not exactly relish the appearance on the screen of his daughter in battle scenes, the millionaire, realizing what his refusal would mean to Mr. Pertell, made no objections. Besides, it was Estelle Brown who was filmed, not Miss Passamore.

"Well, what is next on the program?" asked Alice of the director one day, after several other war plays had been made and when they were about to leave Oak Farm, to go back to New York.

"Oh, I think I'm going to get out a big film entitled 'Life in the Slums.' You and Ruth will play the star parts."

"No!" laughed Alice. "Not since we became millionaires. You will have to cast us for rich girls. Mr. Passamore gave us the ten thousand dollars reward, you know."

"All right!" laughed the director, "then I'll bill you as the rich-poor girls."

Before going back to San Francisco with Mildred, Mr. Passamore had insisted that Ruth and Alice take the reward, as it was through their agency that he received word of his daughter's whereabouts. But Ruth and Alice insisted on sharing their good fortune with their friends in the company, so all benefited from it.

The day came for the moving picture players to leave Oak Farm.

"Good-bye, Sandy!" called Alice to the young farmer. "I suppose you're glad to see the last of us!"

"Well, not exactly, no'm! Still, I'll be glad not to see houses and barns that have only fronts to 'em, and there won't be no more mistakes made trying to haul up water from a well that's only made of painted muslin. I'll try an' get back to real life for a change!"

The big war play was over. It was a big success when shown on the screen, and the pictures of Ruth, Alice and Mildred— or Estelle Brown, as she was billed—came out well. The fight where Paul and his men were nearly blown up was most realistic.

"You girls are not going to retire, just because you have a little money, are you?" asked Russ of Ruth, one day, when they were back in New York.

"Indeed, we're not!" cried Alice. "And I wouldn't be surprised if Mildred joined us. I had a letter from her the other day, and, after seeing herself on the screen, she says she is crazy to do it all over again. Give up the movies? Never!"

And it remains for time to show what further fame the Moving Picture Girls won in the silent drama. For the present, we will say farewell.

ABOUT THE AUTHOR

Laura Lee Hope is a pseudonym used by the Stratemeyer Syndicate for the Bobbsey Twins and several other series of children's novels. Actual writers taking up the pen of Laura Lee Hope include Howard and Lilian Garis, Elizabeth Ward, Harriet (Stratemeyer) Adams, and Nancy Axelrad.

Choose from Thousands of 1stWorldLibrary Classics By

A. M. Barnard
Ada Leverson
Adolphus William Ward
Aesop
Agatha Christie
Alexander Aaronsohn
Alexander Kielland
Alexandre Dumas
Alfred Gatty
Alfred Ollivant
Alice Duer Miller
Alice Turner Curtis
Alice Dunbar
Allen Chapman
Alleyne Ireland
Ambrose Bierce
Amelia E. Barr
Amory H. Bradford
Andrew Lang
Andrew McFarland Davis
Andy Adams
Angela Brazil
Anna Alice Chapin
Anna Sewell
Annie Besant
Annie Hamilton Donnell
Annie Payson Call
Annie Roe Carr
Annonaymous
Anton Chekhov
Archibald Lee Fletcher
Arnold Bennett
Arthur C. Benson
Arthur Conan Doyle
Arthur M. Winfield
Arthur Ransome
Arthur Schnitzler
Arthur Train
Atticus
B.H. Baden-Powell
B. M. Bower
B. C. Chatterjee
Baroness Emmuska Orczy
Baroness Orczy
Basil King
Bayard Taylor
Ben Macomber
Bertha Muzzy Bower
Bjornstjerne Bjornson

Booth Tarkington
Boyd Cable
Bram Stoker
C. Collodi
C. E. Orr
C. M. Ingleby
Carolyn Wells
Catherine Parr Traill
Charles A. Eastman
Charles Amory Beach
Charles Dickens
Charles Dudley Warner
Charles Farrar Browne
Charles Ives
Charles Kingsley
Charles Klein
Charles Hanson Towne
Charles Lathrop Pack
Charles Romyn Dake
Charles Whibley
Charles Willing Beale
Charlotte M. Braeme
Charlotte M. Yonge
Charlotte Perkins Stetson
Clair W. Hayes
Clarence Day Jr.
Clarence E. Mulford
Clemence Housman
Confucius
Coningsby Dawson
Cornelis DeWitt Wilcox
Cyril Burleigh
D. H. Lawrence
Daniel Defoe
David Garnett
Dinah Craik
Don Carlos Janes
Donald Keyhoe
Dorothy Kilner
Dougan Clark
Douglas Fairbanks
E. Nesbit
E. P. Roe
E. Phillips Oppenheim
E. S. Brooks
Earl Barnes
Edgar Rice Burroughs
Edith Van Dyne
Edith Wharton

Edward Everett Hale
Edward J. O'Biren
Edward S. Ellis
Edwin L. Arnold
Eleanor Atkins
Eleanor Hallowell Abbott
Eliot Gregory
Elizabeth Gaskell
Elizabeth McCracken
Elizabeth Von Arnim
Ellem Key
Emerson Hough
Emilie F. Carlen
Emily Bronte
Emily Dickinson
Enid Bagnold
Enilor Macartney Lane
Erasmus W. Jones
Ernie Howard Pie
Ethel May Dell
Ethel Turner
Ethel Watts Mumford
Eugene Sue
Eugenie Foa
Eugene Wood
Eustace Hale Ball
Evelyn Everett-green
Everard Cotes
F. H. Cheley
F. J. Cross
F. Marion Crawford
Fannie E. Newberry
Federick Austin Ogg
Ferdinand Ossendowski
Fergus Hume
Florence A. Kilpatrick
Fremont B. Deering
Francis Bacon
Francis Darwin
Frances Hodgson Burnett
Frances Parkinson Keyes
Frank Gee Patchin
Frank Harris
Frank Jewett Mather
Frank L. Packard
Frank V. Webster
Frederic Stewart Isham
Frederick Trevor Hill
Frederick Winslow Taylor

Friedrich Kerst
Friedrich Nietzsche
Fyodor Dostoyevsky
G.A. Henty
G.K. Chesterton
Gabrielle E. Jackson
Garrett P. Serviss
Gaston Leroux
George A. Warren
George Ade
Geroge Bernard Shaw
George Cary Eggleston
George Durston
George Ebers
George Eliot
George Gissing
George MacDonald
George Meredith
George Orwell
George Sylvester Viereck
George Tucker
George W. Cable
George Wharton James
Gertrude Atherton
Gordon Casserly
Grace E. King
Grace Gallatin
Grace Greenwood
Grant Allen
Guillermo A. Sherwell
Gulielma Zollinger
Gustav Flaubert
H. A. Cody
H. B. Irving
H.C. Bailey
H. G. Wells
H. H. Munro
H. Irving Hancock
H. R. Naylor
H. Rider Haggard
H. W. C. Davis
Haldeman Julius
Hall Caine
Hamilton Wright Mabie
Hans Christian Andersen
Harold Avery
Harold McGrath
Harriet Beecher Stowe
Harry Castlemon
Harry Coghill
Harry Houidini

Hayden Carruth
Helent Hunt Jackson
Helen Nicolay
Hendrik Conscience
Hendy David Thoreau
Henri Barbusse
Henrik Ibsen
Henry Adams
Henry Ford
Henry Frost
Henry James
Henry Jones Ford
Henry Seton Merriman
Henry W Longfellow
Herbert A. Giles
Herbert Carter
Herbert N. Casson
Herman Hesse
Hildegard G. Frey
Homer
Honore De Balzac
Horace B. Day
Horace Walpole
Horatio Alger Jr.
Howard Pyle
Howard R. Garis
Hugh Lofting
Hugh Walpole
Humphry Ward
Ian Maclaren
Inez Haynes Gillmore
Irving Bacheller
Isabel Cecilia Williams
Isabel Hornibrook
Israel Abrahams
Ivan Turgenev
J.G.Austin
J. Henri Fabre
J. M. Barrie
J. M. Walsh
J. Macdonald Oxley
J. R. Miller
J. S. Fletcher
J. S. Knowles
J. Storer Clouston
J. W. Duffield
Jack London
Jacob Abbott
James Allen
James Andrews
James Baldwin

James Branch Cabell
James DeMille
James Joyce
James Lane Allen
James Lane Allen
James Oliver Curwood
James Oppenheim
James Otis
James R. Driscoll
Jane Abbott
Jane Austen
Jane L. Stewart
Janet Aldridge
Jens Peter Jacobsen
Jerome K. Jerome
Jessie Graham Flower
John Buchan
John Burroughs
John Cournos
John F. Kennedy
John Gay
John Glasworthy
John Habberton
John Joy Bell
John Kendrick Bangs
John Milton
John Philip Sousa
John Taintor Foote
Jonas Lauritz Idemil Lie
Jonathan Swift
Joseph A. Altsheler
Joseph Carey
Joseph Conrad
Joseph E. Badger Jr
Joseph Hergesheimer
Joseph Jacobs
Jules Vernes
Julian Hawthrone
Julie A Lippmann
Justin Huntly McCarthy
Kakuzo Okakura
Karle Wilson Baker
Kate Chopin
Kenneth Grahame
Kenneth McGaffey
Kate Langley Bosher
Kate Langley Bosher
Katherine Cecil Thurston
Katherine Stokes
L. A. Abbot
L. T. Meade

L. Frank Baum
Latta Griswold
Laura Dent Crane
Laura Lee Hope
Laurence Housman
Lawrence Beasley
Leo Tolstoy
Leonid Andreyev
Lewis Carroll
Lewis Sperry Chafer
Lilian Bell
Lloyd Osbourne
Louis Hughes
Louis Joseph Vance
Louis Tracy
Louisa May Alcott
Lucy Fitch Perkins
Lucy Maud Montgomery
Luther Benson
Lydia Miller Middleton
Lyndon Orr
M. Corvus
M. H. Adams
Margaret E. Sangster
Margret Howth
Margaret Vandercook
Margaret W. Hungerford
Margret Penrose
Maria Edgeworth
Maria Thompson Daviess
Mariano Azuela
Marion Polk Angellotti
Mark Overton
Mark Twain
Mary Austin
Mary Catherine Crowley
Mary Cole
Mary Hastings Bradley
Mary Roberts Rinehart
Mary Rowlandson
M. Wollstonecraft Shelley
Maud Lindsay
Max Beerbohm
Myra Kelly
Nathaniel Hawthrone
Nicolo Machiavelli
O. F. Walton
Oscar Wilde

Owen Johnson
P.G. Wodehouse
Paul and Mabel Thorne
Paul G. Tomlinson
Paul Severing
Percy Brebner
Percy Keese Fitzhugh
Peter B. Kyne
Plato
Quincy Allen
R. Derby Holmes
R. L. Stevenson
R. S. Ball
Rabindranath Tagore
Rahul Alvares
Ralph Bonehill
Ralph Henry Barbour
Ralph Victor
Ralph Waldo Emmerson
Rene Descartes
Ray Cummings
Rex Beach
Rex E. Beach
Richard Harding Davis
Richard Jefferies
Richard Le Gallienne
Robert Barr
Robert Frost
Robert Gordon Anderson
Robert L. Drake
Robert Lansing
Robert Lynd
Robert Michael Ballantyne
Robert W. Chambers
Rosa Nouchette Carey
Rudyard Kipling
Saint Augustine
Samuel B. Allison
Samuel Hopkins Adams
Sarah Bernhardt
Sarah C. Hallowell
Selma Lagerlof
Sherwood Anderson
Sigmund Freud
Standish O'Grady
Stanley Weyman
Stella Benson
Stella M. Francis

Stephen Crane
Stewart Edward White
Stijn Streuvels
Swami Abhedananda
Swami Parmananda
T. S. Ackland
T. S. Arthur
The Princess Der Ling
Thomas A. Janvier
Thomas A Kempis
Thomas Anderton
Thomas Bailey Aldrich
Thomas Bulfinch
Thomas De Quincey
Thomas Dixon
Thomas H. Huxley
Thomas Hardy
Thomas More
Thornton W. Burgess
U. S. Grant
Upton Sinclair
Valentine Williams
Various Authors
Vaughan Kester
Victor Appleton
Victor G. Durham
Victoria Cross
Virginia Woolf
Wadsworth Camp
Walter Camp
Walter Scott
Washington Irving
Wilbur Lawton
Wilkie Collins
Willa Cather
Willard F. Baker
William Dean Howells
William le Queux
W. Makepeace Thackeray
William W. Walter
William Shakespeare
Winston Churchill
Yei Theodora Ozaki
Yogi Ramacharaka
Young E. Allison
Zane Grey